AF564697

TRIAL COURTS MANAGEMENT

TRIAL COURTS MANAGEMENT

DR. K.L. BHATIA
B.A. (Hons.), LL.M., Ph.D. (Pune)
Professor of Law
(Former Director, The Law School University of Jammu,
Head of the Department of Law,
Dean Faculty of Law, and
Convenor, Board of Studies in Law)

DEEP & DEEP PUBLICATIONS PVT. LTD.
F-159, Rajouri Garden, New Delhi-110027

TRIAL COURTS MANAGEMENT

ISBN 81-7629-873-5

Typeset by ASHISH TECHNOGRAPHICS,
3190, Mohindra Park, Shakur Basti, Delhi-110034.

Printed in India at MAYUR ENTERPRISES,
WZ Plot No. 3, Gujjar Market, Tihar Village, New Delhi-110018.

Published by DEEP & DEEP PUBLICATIONS PVT. LTD.
F-159, Rajouri Garden, New Delhi-110027.
Phones: 25435369, 25440916
E-mail: ddpbooks@yahoo.co.in • deep98@del3.vsnl.net.in
Showroom:
2/13, Ansari Road, Daryaganj, New Delhi-110002 • Telefax: 23245122

DEDICATED IN THE CHERISHED MEMORY OF MY
REVERED MOTHER SWARANA BHATIA,
AAI SMT. RADHA BHATIA AND
BROTHER DEVINDER

Contents

University of Jammu

Jammu - 180006

PROFESSOR AMITABH MATTOO
Vice-Chancellor

Phones: 435268, 450014 (0)
454390, 434339 (R)
Fax: 0191-450014
E-Mail: amitabhmattoo@hotmall.com

Message

In recent years, the idea of good governance has increasingly become one of the most dominant themes in Indian politics. While much of the academic work on the idea of good governance has focused on the role of political leaders and parties and ways, for instance, to reform the bureaucracy, it is clear that an efficient, effective and fair judiciary is essential to any notion of good governance. It is important thus for academics and political thinkers to focus on the judiciary and judicial reforms. I am delighted, therefore, that Prof. K.L. Bhatia has produced a pioneering research study on Courts Management especially in the context of Trial Courts. Any one who has been involved in any significant litigation will recognize the tremendous limitations that Indian Trial Courts suffer from. Therefore, improved court management and case management is essential if the judiciary has not to lose the complete confidence of popular opinion. There could be no better person to undertake this study than Prof. Bhatia. Besides being leading legal thinker and a brilliant teacher, he has also been a superb manager as Director of the newly established The Law School of the University of Jammu. The study is being undertaken with the rigor of a good social scientist with a clear research design, hypothesis and methodology. I have no doubt that it will become one of the definitive works on the subject.

Amitabh Mattoo

AMITABH MATTOO

Justice R.P. Sethi
Former Judge
Supreme Court of India

Phones: 0191-2586877
0191-2572894, 2547616
Ext.: 23-24 Off.: Ext.-27
Fax: 0191-2574666
E-mail:

Foreword

Huge pendency, the serpent like long queue from Kashmir to Kanyakumari of the seekers of justice and the Everest touching arrears of cases pending in the Trial Courts of the country is not only alarming but in fact likely to endanger and shake the confidence of the people in the so far most respected institution of judiciary. According to the information available about 2.5 crore cases are pending in the District Courts of the country, of which about 1.5 crores are criminal cases. Cases arising out of the cognizable offences under the IPC alone are 49,21,710 and more than 37,00,000 under the special laws. The conviction rate in criminal cases is less than 7% and the disposal rate of cases pending in the Courts is much on the lower side as compared to the institutions. Despite numerous reports of the Law Commission, the recommendations in the form of observations in the verdicts of the Apex and the High Courts and the reports of special Committees and Commissions constituted for the purpose, there does not appear to be any immediate hope of meeting the challenge of reducing the arrears of pending cases.

To overcome the uphill task, there are various proposed methods of far reaching effect for permanently dealing with the challenge, which include the change in the prevalent judicial system in the country, increase in the strength of the Judges and the Courts, to resort to alternative redressal system of judicial dispensation, to restrict the right of appeal and revisions etc. There are also short-term measures, which under the prevalent system of justice are considered inevitable to make efforts for overcoming and reducing the pendency of cases in the subordinate Courts of the country. The most important short-term inexpensive measure is the proper Court and Case Management. The ambit and scope of Court Management relates to managing the cause list, understanding in detail the facts and law applicable in each case, docket management, controlling and managing adjournments, a firm grip on record system, discipline over the Court staff, study of case law by the presiding Judges, effectively controlling the grant of interim measures in pending cases, resort to conciliation, mediation, legal-aid, Lok-adalats and arbitrations, furnishing of data regarding the institution and disposal of cases to the higher Courts and the like. The experience has shown that the system has become the sufferer. The consumers of justice are the victims of the apathy of the trial Courts in dealing with and disposing of expeditiously the matters pending on their boards for decades. The lack of understanding of the Court and Case Management has further deteriorated the worsening conditions of the pendency in the Law Courts of the country.

Neither the supervising Courts, nor the Government appears to have taken any interest in making the judicial dispensation system effective by resorting to interim measures like making the presiding Officer understand the better management of Courts and Cases. Various judicial academies established in the country have been stressing more on the academic aspect of the legal system and appear to be having least interest in studying the shortcomings and the necessity. of improvement in the Court and Case Management.

Prof. K.L. Bhatia deserves all appreciations for making first ever indepth study of Trial Court Management. He has dealt with all aspects, which affect the judicial system as prevalent and practiced by Trial Courts in the country. He has worked hard to collect the best of the material from the Trial Courts pertaining to the causes which have adversely affected the proper Court Management and Case Management. He has studied all human resources in the context of Court Management as according to him new approach on the subject is the need of the hour because antiquated methods have proved to be suicidal for decision-making process by the Courts. He has dealt in detail with the dispensers of justice, the legal system practiced in the subordinate Courts, procedural wrangles which effect the system and pointed out the contours of Court Management before suggesting remedial measures.

It is hoped that both the consumers and dispensers of justice as also all concerned with the establishment of the rule of law in the country would be benefited by this research work. Realizing and understanding the concept of Court and Case Management would help the judiciary, the Bar and the Government in their sincere efforts of reducing the pending arrears in the Trial Courts. The data and information collected, the defects highlighted and the method of improvement shown is sure to help the system in preserving and maintaining its respect, dignity and honour and of inspiring the confidence of the common man in the institution of the judiciary.

JUSTICE R.P. SETHI

Preface

Trial Courts Management is a study of structural understanding of the trial courts. The trial judiciary is confronted with strains such as judicial transparency, judicial independence, judicial attitude and judicial credibility in all perspectives. There may be many vices or agents working against the trial judiciary besides delay that is inherent and exorbitant litigation expenses. These may relate to court management and case management; indecisiveness; disinterestedness; juristocratic recidivist attitude/behaviour to the disposal of cases; corruption; justice perceptions and visions.

The idea of court management and case management concerns the trial judges who have to be "trial judiciary managerial" that ultimately have to instill confidence in "justice seekers" that "justice dispensers" are indeed "justice conceivers". The trial court judges, in this way, therefore, are required to become "Trial Managers", "Interventionists", "Dispensers of Justice", rather than mere "Neutral Umpires". Unfortunately, the concept of court management and case management has not yet made inroads in the road-map of law reforms. Be that as it may, we must not make a scarecrow of it. Court management and case management in essence mean decision-making process of the trial judiciary to arrive at just ends by just means and as such imperative in the trial judicial system in India. It has been endeavoured to have in depth insights into the notions of court management and case management. Court management is an administrative tool in how the courts control the case management; it is an aspect of the court taking over the management of the case. Case management has varied contours, namely, how the information is controlled, how the cases get filed, how the cases processed through the courts, how the courts keep track of cases, how Advocates get information about the status of their cases, how "trial courts automation" is maintained. Both court management and case management shall help the trial judges to start to take more active role in the administration of decision-making process where justice delivery system shall appear to be swift and just. That is only possible if certain level of efficiency in trial court judges is addressed in-as-much as that litigation would be under a "start-to-finish" time-table framework, say, 20 to 30 weeks or so. This renaissance/revival culture may help to reduce costs of litigation and minimize delays in trial courts. Unequivocally, the trial judges have to comprehend all the ramifications of modern scientific methods of management of the court system to bring anew court management and case management culture in the trial judiciary lest the system becomes bankrupt.

Research studies on court management and case management are minimal, and it has also not attracted the attention of the researchers, perhaps, due to different perceptions concerning the tale of the legal profession, viz., more "profit oriented" and less "service oriented".

I am indebted to many who gave me the benefit of their scholastic critique counsel in many ways. The successful culmination of the research study has been possible only due to the partial financial assistance of the UGC. There is some delay in the presentation of final results of this research work. The occurrence of delay has been unavoidable, first, due to belated responses from the respondents (trial court judges), secondly, due to my academic as well as administrative pre-occupations, and, thirdly, procourante like situations. I did not like to present half-baked results, and as such consumption of little more time than allotted in the presentation of the final version of the responses. I am, therefore, immensely beholden to the UGC for bearing with me.

My special gratitude is to Justice R.P. Sethi, former Judge, Supreme Court of India, and Professor Amitabh Mattoo, Vice-Chancellor, University of Jammu, who acceded to my request to record their impressions by way of a Foreword and a Message to this book.

I must appreciate the untiring efforts of Mr. Sunil Sharma who has helped me to collect data from the trial courts judges for the successful culmination of this study work. Had he not toiled for it, it could not have been possible for me to bring out the results in the present form.

I am very happy to express my warmest thanks to Professor Dr. S.M. Dahiwale, Department of Sociology, University of Poona, Pune, for his commendable suggestions in the questionnaire, and Mrs. Roshan Dalvi, Judge, Bombay City Civil and Sessions Court, Mumbai, for facilitating the availability of a copy of Justice Shetty Commission Report which has been of immense use in the completion of this study.

My special note of appreciation for my research scholars and colleagues Dr. Sanjay Gupta, Dr. Ms. Renu Jamwal and Mr. Satinder Kumar for extending their selfless help to me in tabulating the data and reducing it to statistical form.

I am immensely beholden to all those Trial Courts Judges who were kind enough to respond to the questionnaire by recording their impressions fairly and fearlessly, because without their responses it could not have been possible to culminate it successfully in enormous "re-acculturation".

Lastly, I must not end without a reference to the unfailing support, encouragement, nourishment of innovative ideas, inspiration, love, and untiring help of my wife Veenal, and two children, Sumeet, an Advocate at Delhi and Manu, a Post-Graduate student, in more ways than I can mention. These few words cannot acknowledge my debt to them and the sociological sentiments, emotions, and ties of affection that make this debt so pleasant to bear with.

Finally, I unhesitatingly acknowledge with thanks to Sh. G.S. Bhatia, Deep & Deep Publications Pvt. Ltd., New Delhi to bring this book within neat time.

Jammu

PROF. K.L. BHATIA

Judicial Colloquia on "Trial Court Management" presented by the author High Court, Jammu

Judicial Colloquia on "Trial Court Management". High Court, Jammu

Lok Adalat act D & S Judge Jammu

Judicial Colloquia on "Trial Court Management". High Court, Jammu

Judicial Colloquia on "Trial Court Management". High Court, Jammu

Judicial Colloquia on "Trial Court Management". High Court, Jammu

Judicial Colloquia on "Trial Court Management". High Court, Jammu

Old Complex Courts Mubarik Mandi, Jammu

District Court Bar Members Panchkula

Bar Members
Pathankot

Hind Advocates
Panchkula

D and S Court
Haridwar

Lower Court, Haridwar

Old Complex Dist. and S. Judge Jammu

Old Anti Corruption Judge and other Courts Complex, Mubarik Mandi, Jammu

Old Court Complex, Haridwar

Dist. Court Complex Karkardooma

Dist. Court Complex Karkardooma

Dist. and S.J. Rajouri (J & K)

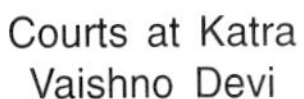

Courts at Katra Vaishno Devi

Lawyer's Chamber, Haridwar (Uttaranchal Pradesh)

Lawyer's Chambers Haridwar

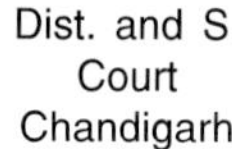

Dist. and S. Court Chandigarh

Dist. Court, Chandigarh Punjab and Haryana

Lawyer's Chamber Panchkula (Haryana)

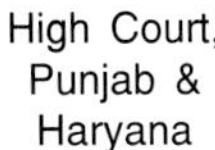

High Court, Punjab & Haryana

Courts at Katra, Vaishno Devi Ji

Trial Courts, Rajouri (J & K)

High Court Complex, Shimla

CAT and D & S Court Chandigarh

District Court Complex Panchkula

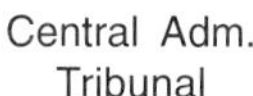

Central Adm. Tribunal

Lawyer's Chambers, Haridwar

Lawyer's Chamber Haridwar

Trial Courts, Roshnabad, Haridwar (Uttaranchal)

Court Complex, Chandigarh

High Court,
New Delhi

Tis Hazari
Court Complex
New Delhi

Patiala House,
New Delhi

Trial Courts at Shimla, Himachal Pradesh

Trial Courts at Himachal Pradesh (Shimla)

High Court Punjab and Haryana

High Court Complex
Shimla

High Court
Himachal Pradesh
(Shimla)

D & S Court
Roshnabad
(Haridwar)

District Court, Punjab & Haryana

District Court (Panchkula) Haryana

1

Introduction

The research study is a study of "Court Management", it is a study of "structural understanding" as observed by the then Justice of the Apex Court of the country Shri P.B. Sawant, viz., "like any other human agency the judiciary has to be under close and constant scrutiny". Court management depends upon various as well as varied factors/faculties/variables. It is observed that better the scope for the efficient as well as quick disposal of cases and lessening or minimizing the delay in the disposal of cases as the tendency to decide important questions of law and life by judicial fiat seems to be on the increase in India, given the fact and perceptions of the ever increasing arrears and work load.[1] At the outset it may be stated that the insights gained in an in depth study of trial courts would, indeed, help to have deep 'insights' into the "strains confronting the subordinate judiciary in the country" as well as judicial transparency, judicial independence, judicial attitude and judicial credibility in all perspectives. What we need is worthwhile empirical studies to bridge a gap in our knowledge, which ought really to be remedied sooner than later. The state of "trial courts (subordinate judiciary) is the mirror of the governance of the State or the country". (Per C.J. E.S. Venkataramiah).

---

1. See Upendra Baxi, The Crisis of the Indian Legal System, 1982.

In the backdrop of the above, there seems to be some penetrating questions around the trial courts functioning in quest of some justifiable answers. Why there are so many infernos around the trial judiciary? Why the trial judiciary is in the ocean of anguish? What for to blame the trial judiciary? Is it in the conflict between justice and justices? The trial judiciary certainly cannot be free from immunity from the criticism and controversy of these contentious, there is nothing pretentious about it, inquisitives. The reaction to the criticism and controversy may be attributed to the reaction of Voltaire that twice in life he was ruined, first time when he lost the litigation and second time, when he won it.[2] It may too safely be attributed to Pandit Jawaharlal Nehru who because of his experience and not of (hate) opposition *a multo fortiori* observed: "The defect really lies with the judicial structure that we have inherited from the British (colonial or common law system) which entails inordinate delay and expense. However, efficacious the system may be, it really proves to be unjust in the end because of the excessive delay and expense it involves."[3]

Besides, it seems that there is unhappiness against the trial judiciary. Why? Where does lie the cause is nobody's concern? But still unhappiness is expressed with full volume. Be that as it may, there may be many vices or agents working against the trial judiciary besides delay and exorbitant expenses. These may relate to Court Management as well as Case Management; indecisiveness; disinterestedness; juristocratic recidivist attitude/behaviour to

2. See N.A. Palkhiwala, We the People, p. 341.
3. See Rajiv Dhavan and Thomas Paul, Nehru and the Constitution, Indian Law Institute, 1992, p. 73; 117th Law Commission of India Report, Training of Judicial Officers, 1986, p. 1 : "Indian Judicial System is admittedly colonial in origin and imported in structure. Without even a semblance of change . . . since independence, in its mode, method of work, designations, language, approach, method of resolving disputes, it has all the trappings of the system established by the foreign rulers"; The Administration of Justice in India in its structure and organization has the stamp of "Made in U.K.": See 131st Report of the Law Commission of India, Role of the Legal Profession in Administration of Justice, 1988, p. 1.

the disposal of cases; corruption; justice perceptions and visions.

COURT MANAGEMENT AND CASE MANAGEMENT

Court management and case management is a boon of the justice delivery system. It relates to the idea of the trial judges being "trial judiciary managerial" to instill confidence in "justice seekers" that "justice dispensers" are indeed "justice conceivers". Unfortunately, the concept of court management and case management has not yet made inroads in the roadmap of law reforms. Perhaps, lawmen do not take the strides of law reforms seriously, because "they think the law exists as the atmosphere exists, and the notion that could be improved is too startling to entertain".[4] Or, it may be as Francis Bacon gives vent to: "Judges must beware of hard constructions and strained interferences; for there is no worse torture than the torture of laws".[5] Or, as Shakespeare spells: "Look with thine ears: see how yond justice rails upon yond simple thief. Hark, in thine ears: change places; and, handy-dandy, which is the justice, which is the thief."[6] Or, as Newton Minow echoes in the same vein: "In Germany, under the law everything is prohibited except that which is permitted. In France, everything is permitted except that which is prohibited. In the Soviet Union, everything is prohibited, including that which is permitted. And in Italy, under the law everything is permitted, especially that which is prohibited."[7] Though court management and case management appear to be imperative in trial judiciary, but the reforms in this perspective shall only catch the attention when the things are worst enough already for reforms.[8] The

---

4. Per Lord Goodman (1913-1995) as quoted by Ronald Irving, The Law is a Ass, the first Indian reprint, 2002, p. 54.
5. Francis Bacon, *'Of Judicature'*, Essays, LVI, 1625.
6. William Shakespeare (1564-1616), King Lear, 4.6, (1605-06).
7. Newton Minow, *A Comparative Study of Legal Systems, Times Magazine,*18 March 1985, as quoted in The Law is as Ass, *op. cit.*
8. Vide Lord Justice Astbury (1866-1939), as quoted in The Law is a Ass, *op. cit.* p. 49.

perceptions concerning court management and case management are not conceived alarming yet because of the dogmatic perceptions: "One of the greatest delusions in the world is the hope that the evils of this world can be cured by legislation."[9]

Be that as it may, 'we must not make a scarecrow of the law'. Court management and case management is inasmuch as imperative for reforms in the Trial Judicial System in India as the developed western countries like U.S.A. and U.K. have faced the flak. Court management and case management in essence mean decision-making process of the trial judiciary to arrive at just ends by just means. Court management is an administrative tool in how the courts control the case management;[10] it is an aspect of the court taking over the management of the case.[11] Case management, according to Judge Ms Fern M. Smith, has varied contours: how the information is controlled, how the cases get filed, how the cases proceed through the courts, how the courts keep track of cases, how attorneys get information about the status of their cases.[12] Court management and case management requires two pronged strategies to streamline the trial judiciary, viz., the "Trial Courts Automation", and trial courts ability and willingness to step in and basically take charge of the cases themselves.[13] This what the trial courts in the United States have started doing since 1990 with the enforcement of the Civil Justice Reform Act of 1990.[14] Since then the trial judges started taking more active role in the administration of "decision making process" of the trial judiciary; they also started reporting the Congress about how long cases were taking to get through; they also set the

---

9. Thomas B. Reed (1839-1902), *US Lawyer and Politician*, as quoted in The Law is a Ass, *op. cit.*, p. 49.
10. Judge Ms Fern M. Smith, Director of the Federal Judicial Center, Washington, *Educating the Judiciary*, *Span*, January-February, 2001, p. 16.
11. Lord Justice Woolf's Report, Access to Justice, July 26, 1996.
12. *Ibid.*
13. *Ibid.*
14. *Ibid.*

schedules of the cases for their expeditious disposal by actively stepping in and basically taking charge of the cases themselves.[15] Trial (Federal) courts automation has indeed made a huge impact in the way cases are perceived in the courtrooms.[16] There is a great impetus of the Human Resource Development in the judicial process. Computers have been playing a tremendous role in easing the burden, in freeing up the staff from very tedious, hand recording of documents; computers have freed up space because the mound of papers is reduced substantially.[17]

Automation of the trial judiciary, this way, has revolutionized the decision making process in the United States. For example, documents now come in through computers and on screens; lawyers keep track of their documents on computers which they bring to the court room; lawyers now could walk in the court room with their laptop and try a case without a piece of paper just by pulling up the documents they needed on their laptop and having them illustrated in front of a trial judge.[18] Computing technology has also equally done to the substantive law, viz., computing technology has become the driving force of the American economy—E-Commerce, cyber commerce and software.[19] In almost all the legal firms in the States now this computing economy is the focus of their practice,[20] namely, the cases involve cyber law issues, patents on computers, copyright on software, information technology management, etc.[21] A new wonderful way of saving costs and time making things more efficient in the trial judiciary is the introduction of "video conference" an innovative way to conduct hearings and examine witnesses, namely, trial of cases by people who may not even be in the court room. "Video conference hearings"

15. *Ibid.*
16. *Ibid.*
17. *Ibid.*
18. *Ibid.*
19. *Ibid.*
20. *Ibid.*
21. *Ibid.*

take place with the attorneys present on the video screen who are actually sitting all over the country and witnesses thousands of kilometers away will appear on a video screen, and a judge may perhaps be sitting in one city with all the witnesses and all the attorneys sitting in another city.[22] "Video conference hearings" may not be free from problems, but that need not be impediments in the managerial process of the trial judiciary. However, in this computing set up in the trial judiciary the increased role of expert witnesses is imperative, and the need for trial judges to be scientifically and technologically aware. Besides, the court management and case management also requires the skills of trial judiciary to resorting to "Alternative Disputes Resolutions", and/or "Mediation Process", viz., to find quick and inexpensive ways to resolve cases without every case needing to go through full court process.[23]

The main thrust of court management and case management in the U.K., like the United States, as advocated by Lord Justice Woolf in its Report of 1966 is that courts are required to be managed as present day industry and trade, namely, a determined effort to make justice cheaper, speedier and easier to obtain, and to make the judicial delivery system simpler, more flexible and more accessible.[24] This involves three pronged strategies:

- Increasing the resources for handling present cases;
- Reducing the number of cases entering the system;
- Improving the system of handling cases that have already entered the system.[25]

The trial court judges are required to become "Trial Managers", "Interventionists", "Dispensers of Justice", rather

22. *Ibid.*
23. *Ibid.*
24. Lord Justice Woolf's Report, July 26, 1966, Access to Justice; M.A. Khan (Registrar Delhi H.C.) and Ms Roshan Dalvi (Judge, Bombay City Civil and Sessions Court), 1997 (Unpublished).
25. *Ibid.*

than mere "Neutral Umpires". Court management and case management require 'certain level of efficiency in trial court Judges' in-as-much as that' litigation would be under a "start-to-finish" time-table of 20 to 30 weeks'.[26] This may bring Civil Justice Revolution, reducing costs and minimizing delays in trial courts.[27] The trial court Judge would thus be in the "driving seat" and by applying his managerial skills involve transfer of control from the parties in an adversarial system to the Judge, designed to end "trial by combat".[28] The Report *a fortiori* states that it shall naturally have its impetus on Barristers, Solicitors, Judges, Staff as well as the court itself and culminating in enormous "re-acculturation".[29] Lord Woolf's Report emphasizes that in court management and case management the most important aspect is "tracking" and the "managing Judge" has an important role to play, viz.,

Fast Track: The court management and case management would involve what is stated to be "front loading litigation" involving collection of documentation, witnesses, experts and issues as soon as the litigation is filed.[30]

Multi Track: Litigation involving upwards amount, the trial Judge would have the discretion to decide, tailored to the needs of the individual case, to what extent it could be automated, upon holding a Case Management Conference after the defense has been filed to hone down the issues and enable the litigants, in the participatory approach, to form better informed decisions and exert more control over what is done on their behalf.[31]

In the backdrop of the above, the following interests, as per Woolf's Report, come within the purview of court management and case management:

- Private Interest

26. *Ibid.*
27. *Ibid.*
28. *Ibid.*
29. *Ibid.*
30. *Ibid.*
31. *Ibid.*

- Public Interest
- Private and Public Interest
- Outcome Related Interest.

Court management and case management also involves for improved litigation culture, that is, the active involvement of the "Managerial Judge" taking control of the litigation and deciding whether "Alternative Disputes Resolution" or "Mediation" is imperative in the decision-making process of the trial judiciary. This aspect is called as "Appropriate Dispute Resolution" ("A.D.R.")[32], and as such involves

- Planning
- Time Scale
- Realistic and expeditious time table
- Cost Tracking
- Cost Limitation

This thus involves an innovative litigious culture in the decision-making process to strengthen court management and case management *de novo* such as:

- Length of time for litigation;
- Cutting down on hearing time;
- Summary procedure;
- Defining important issues;
- Listing of cases;
- Alternative Dispute Resolution;
- Judicial Team.[33]

This all depends upon the managerial skills of the trial Judge to budget the schedule in the decision-making process of the trial courts to "keep the proceedings under his control with a deep commitment to render speedy justice so that the adversarial litigation culture yields to co-operative litigation culture to bring about effective case management. By

32. *Ibid.*
33. *Ibid.*

employing effective managerial techniques, the twin problems of docket explosion and mounting arrears in our already burdened courts can be controlled".[34]

For speedy as well as effective justice a better management of courts device needs to be devised, because it is the only main challenge with which the trial Judiciary in India is faced.[35] Besides the huge arrears of cases pending at different levels in the Trial Courts in India, the adversary system, procedural wrangles and multiplicity of appeals/ revisions/reviews are some of the factors which leave a litigant a bitter and frustrated man while waiting for justice for years.[36] How to overcome these judicial bottlenecks? How to ease judicial-litigant frustrations? These questions intimately concern the devises of better court management and case management as an independent institution of "justice service oriented" character. Unfortunately, this area has been generally ignored in India's Planning roadmap, or the problem of management of courts and cases has not been properly addressed.[37] What has been debated so far in Parliament and in public is concerning the scandalous delays in judicial administration, and such debates have not given the necessary impetus either for a comprehensive restructuring of judicial administration or for better court management and case management as well as Human Resources in judicial process/decision making process.[38] Inescapably, the searching answer to such a question is both political as well as technical.

Political does not mean to criticize any government, but, broadly speaking, it may be overall lack of political will or zeal or attention to address the problem on the part of

34. *Ibid.*
35. See 129th Report of The Law Commission of India on Urban Litigation Mediation as Alternative to Adjudication, 1988, p. 50.
36. *Ibid.*
37. See 120th Report of The Law Commission of India on Manpower Planning in Judiciary: A Blueprint, 1987, p. 1.
38. *Ibid.*; see also M.P. Jain, Outlines of Indian Legal History, 1981, pp. 254-56.

political parties, free press, social activists and the Bar.[39] It may also be argued that the non-effective measures in this perspective have been largely due to the factor that the Indian state since the colonial period has self-consciously under-staffed the judiciary; and, even after the Independence, too, this colonial legacy-situation has been allowed to perpetuate.[40] The reasons for this are not far to seek. Be that as it may, lack of effective will to campaign for adequate manpower planning or extending the application of human resource development concepts to the Indian judiciary speak volumes and shows apathy of the concerns towards the development of this justice delivery institution. This is called technical reason, namely, the developing science of human resource development or manpower planning has not attracted the attention of policy conceivers, policy opinion makers in the area of court management and case management as well as administration of justice in India.[41] What ought to be the scientific and systematic solution to the court management and case management problem? This needs to be addressed to some searching questions in order to arrive at some meaningful results, such as: (a) On what principles have decisions been taken concerning the appropriate strength in each cadre of the Judiciary?; (b) Have these principles or norms ever been publicly debated, if not, is court management and case management secret institution?; (c) Have these principles changed since Independence, and, if changed, with what impetus?; (d) The burden of the Trial Judiciary has increased with the introduction of new nature of causes and offences with the passage of new legislations (POTA, FEMA, TRIP, etc.) since Independence. The penetrating question is: Does the Law and Justice Department of the Ministry of Law, Justice and Company Affairs keep the proportional increase in the workload of Trial Courts in mind and proposes any corresponding increase in money and manpower of the Trial Judiciary while creating new causes

39. See 120th Report of The Law Commission of India, *op. cit.*
40. *Ibid.*
41. *Ibid.*

and offences? Do the Law and Justice Department make any manpower planning for the Trial Judiciary? Unfortunately, these questions have not properly and adequately been addressed from behavioural perspectives "which are inimical to development of sound administration of justice"[42] culture at the Trial Judiciary in India, and as such an in depth study, understanding and examination of such inquisitive questions is imperative for comparative scientific analysis.

Human resource Development is *sine qua non* judicial process, viz., court management and case management. The contours of court management and case management relate to: (i) Docket management (arrears and delay); (ii) Records systems; (iii) Discipline over non-judicial staff; (iv) Cases and library automation (computerized management and Information Retrieval to the extent applicable); (v) Management of *Ex-parte,* Stay, Interim Orders; (vi) Management of adjournment motions; (vii) Monitoring judicial performance; (viii) Management of Legal Aid, Lok Adalats, Alternative Disputes Resolution; (ix) Management of Feedback to High Courts; (x) Systems Management, namely, understanding of the law as a mutually intricating cultural, institutional, behavioural system, and systematic interaction of the Trial Judge with jail, Police, Bar, Legal activists, social activists, *Pro Bono Publico,* Law Schools/Institutions/ Universities, High Court, etc.

In the backdrop of the above, human resources in the context of court management and case management seems to be critical because the "quality and quantity of human resources significantly influence the level of effectiveness as well as efficiency of the people who operate",[43] the trial judiciary. And as such, court management and case management in judicial process as are keenly felt, because antiquated methods are suicidal for the decision making processes in this age of 21st century where "sociology of law is acquiring new and added significance in the development

42. *Ibid.*

43. See 117th Report of The Law Commission of India, Training of Judicial Officers, 1986, p. 1.

of the society".[44] Therefore, knowledge, skills, and attitudes in lawmen require to be sharpened to bring anew court management and case management culture in the trial judiciary. If justice is the hallmark of courts then a new manpower planning in the trial judiciary has to be strived. Unequivocally, the trial judges have to undertake the management of court and justice system; they have to undertake training in modern methods of management of the court and court system lest the system becomes bankrupt; they have to comprehend all the ramifications of the system that an administrative decision might bring about; there has to be court automation at war footing as computers can increase efficiency in the area of court calendaring since congested and conflicting court calendars cause delay in court proceedings; court automation cannot only be used to improve the clerical culture/aptitude/attitude of judicial administration but also to retrieve case law and statutory material.[45]

Research studies on court management and case management are minimal, and it has also not attracted the attention of the researchers perhaps due to different perceptions concerning the tale of the legal profession which seems to be conceded by the critics "no longer service-oriented (but) it is only profit oriented, and that the lawyers are out only to squeeze the clients to the maximum extent possible ... and the contemporary legal profession has fallen in the popular estimation because of the greed for money, lengthening of the case for years together for small reasons and even changing their loyalty to the other party for the sake of money only. Sometimes, Lawyers of both sides join hands to make both the parties compromise even if the clients have to suffer the loss. Majority of the lawyers harass

---

44. *Id.*, p. 2; 131st report of the Law Commission of India, Role of the Legal Profession in Administration of Justice, 1987, p. 1: "If little sociology leads one away from the law, much sociology returns one to the study of the law".
45. See 127th Report of The Law Commission of India, Resource Allocation for Infra-structure Services in Judicial Administration, 1988, pp. 1, 3, 15. 16, 17.

their clients for more and more fees, false bills while not taking the required interest in the case".[46]

There is a complaint by the public, jurists and Bar against the judicial system of the country. Such complaints are based on facts that "higher courts are right because they are superior, not superior because they are right"[47]; higher courts literally operate "in a goldfish bowl";[48] judicial decisions, particularly in the superior courts and multi-judge appellate courts, are collegial, incremental, and reached in an atmosphere that justice Lewis Powell has described as one of "the last citadels of jealously preserved individualism," and, such a perception may be on account of jurisprudential truth that "law is a jealous lady". Courts like the other branches of the government belong to the Indian people. "An independent judiciary need not be a mysterious area of government or appear to be an occult priesthood or remain a remote, austere marble temple housing ... seldom seen jurists who periodically issue pronouncements on the law of the land".[49]

RESEARCH PROBLEM

The Law Commission of India in its various reports, as already discussed above, and also Justice V.S. Malimath in his report have made scathing criticism against the functioning of the higher judiciary which ultimately culminates into delayed justice. Delay can be termed as a fountainhead of indecisiveness causes unpleasantness. It is surmising that no study in the country has been conducted on trial judges and the adversarial process. The role and responsibilities of trial judges are often underestimated and neglected, perhaps, because, trial courts are but the first tier in the judicial system, or, because of an upper court bias. We read and hear more about appellate courts especially the Supreme Court,

46. See 131st Report of The Law Commission of India, *op.cit.*, p. 8.
47. Frank M. Coffin, Views from the Bench, 1987, p. 27.
48. *Id.*, *xi.*
49. C.I. U.S. Supreme Court : Warren E. Burger

still the trial judges, in fact, handle the bulk of judicial business.

It is argued that justices are engrossed in the confirming task of deciding cases and writing prolific opinions and as such unwilling remoteness may occur. It may, however, be not conceived that they do not want people to understand the judicial function in our system; unfortunately, there are relatively few people to understand, interpret and explain the court's role in wider terms. In a sense people know less about the courts than they do about the Parliament or political parties. People may have a lot of mistaken views about the Parliament and the political parties, but the problem with the courts is that they are so mysterious. Whatever mystery surrounds the judiciary undoubtedly stems from what Judge Jirome Frank calls "the cult of the role", or Justice Felix Frankfurter felicitously describes as "Judicial lockjaw", or Justice Charles Evans Hughes characterized as "self-inflicted wounds."

Be that as it may, "we are very quiet here, but it is the quiet of a storm center." Courts, as Justice Oliver Wendell Holmes observed are indeed a storm center facing the panoply of human problems, and unrelenting work schedule. Moreover, in Justice Bejemin Cardozo's memorable words "the great tides and currents which engulf the rest of men, do not turn aside in their course, and pass judges by." Trial judges, in fact, handle the bulk of judicial business. Because lower court judges preside over trials among other things—including management of case processing, approval of plea bargains, supervision of the settlement process, and monitoring remedial decrees—they, to a greater degree than appellate judges, experience the drama of adversary process. This inevitably influences judicial decision-making process and behaviour pattern. A (trial) judge is not a mechanical scale or computer. Trial judges, being human, very in their respective qualities of intelligence, perspectiveness, attentiveness—and other mental and emotional characteristics operative while they are listening to, and observing witnesses. After presiding over a trial and reflecting on the evidence and law, the judge *"experienceas a gestalt"* on which he renders a final decision and then may rationalize in a written opinion. However, "no judge writes on a wholly clean slate."

There is an unhappy wide consensus that excellent trial judges are not in long supply. The causes may be identifiable as (a) the difficulty of knowing in advance who will turn out to be a good judge, (b) difficulty concerning the most effective means of selection, and (c) our lack of steady determination to do the things necessary,—e.g., to stop judgeship for patronage—to select the people most likely to be now suitable.

While we fail too regularly to people the bench ideally, the ideal is not itself very uncertain. The qualities which we desire in our trial judge ought to be neutral, detached, kindly, benign, reasonably learned in law, firm but fair, wise, knowledgeable about human behaviour, and, somewhat superhuman. Be that as it may, the qualities in the terms of personality of the trial judge may be succinctly stated as his eight virtues (because none would like to see the reverse of it in a trial judge): independence, courtesy and patience, dignity (but not excluding humour), open-mindedness, impartiality, thoroughness and decisiveness, an understanding heart, and social consciousness. However, there may be variations, but, a central core of agreed standard defines the trial judge as the neutral, impartial, calm, no contentious umpire standing between the adversary parties, seeing that they observe the rules of the adversary game. The bedrock premise is that the adversary contest is the ideal way to achieve truth and a just result rested upon the truth. It is said that the trial judge has a more robust part. The essence of the (trial) judicial role is impartiality and detachment, both felt and exhibited. In the quest for truth through the clash of contradictions, which is, of course the only reason in theory for having trials, the judge does not care where the chips may fell. Concerned only that the right is done, the (trial) judge "should be patient, dignified, and courteous to litigants, witnesses, lawyers, and others" as he presides over the contentious strivings towards that end.

These are banalities. Nevertheless, the fact is that the professed ideals, like others, seem not to be designed, under out practice, for consistently effective pursuits. The tension between the ideals and some insistent realities triggers conflicts. It, therefore, seems expedient imperative that introspection as well as self correction at the level of subordinate judiciary is the need of the hour; and that, perhaps, is the instrument prompting to take up an in depth study of the conceived problem scientifically and systematically. The role of the trial judge and the adversarial process emanate from different factors such as (a) trial judges strength and manpower, (b) ministerial staff attached with the trial judges, (c) budgetary allocations in favour of trial courts, (d) physical equipments, (f) role of the trial judge to the proclaimed virtues, (g) role of the members of the Bar to the proclaimed virtues, and, lastly (h) the personal aptitude of the trial judge.

OBJECTIVES

The research problem thus conceived addresses itself to understanding in depth the :

(I) Working of the trial courts in the country;

(II) Interaction and interdependence of the trial courts, lawyers, Higher Court, litigants, non-litigants, touts, court-men, investigative agencies;

(III) Rate of disposal of cases/suits per trial judge annually;

(IV) Man days in the court process;

(V) Budgetary allocation and freedom of economic dependence;

(VI) Effective role of supervisory jurisdiction of the State(s) high court(s);

(VII) Mode of selection of trial judges and its efficacy;

(VIII) Physical facilities made available to the trial judges in terms of emoluments, housing, transportation, medical, leave travel concession, library, etc.;

(IX) The modern equipments available in the trial courts for expeditious and judicious disposal of cases, viz., word processors, computers, electronic typewriters, e-commerce, internet, etc.;

(X) Holidays (approved and non-approved) observed;

(XI) Effect of strike by lawyers and man days lost;
(XII) Legal aid and advice process followed vehemently to its spirit and logical conclusion;
(XIII) Causation of delay and piling of cases.

HYPOTHESES

The research study has been conducted keeping in view the under mentioned hypotheses. The testing of these hypotheses would alone tell whether the complaint about the trial courts is genuine one or specious only.

(I) There is sufficient/adequate/ample manpower to dispose of the workload at the trial courts.
(II) The trial courts are so mysterious that they are only beloved in ignorance.
(III) Denied the power of both sword and the purse, the court depends on the cooperation of the coequal branches of government and ultimately public acceptance.
(IV) The trial courts work in a conducive atmosphere because they have ample infrastructure in terms of physical facilities.
(V) The trial courts work conscientiously and efficiently because they have adequate budgetary allocation.
(VI) The trial courts are decisive because only competent judges are selected to the job.
(VII) The trial judges observe punctuality of time.
(VIII) The disposal rate of cases at trial courts level is strictly adhered to because of conducive infrastructure in the form of scientific equipments made available.
(IX) Regular and frequent visits of judges of High Court (including Chief Justice) keep the trial judges disciplined.

Besides the above mentioned hypotheses, it has also been aspired to examine by conducting physical surveys in depth the research question concerning the court room atmosphere and environment, origin of terrorism against judges and advocates in the courts and the protection to the witnesses; when trial courts fail to bring thousands of undertrials to trials for cruelly long periods of time.

RESEARCH METHODOLOGY

(a) Sampling: Universe, Respondents

The research study is fit to be conducted in the whole of the country. In order to arrive at empirical generalizations it means that the ideal situation for empirical generalizations would be the wholesale subordinate courts in the country. But that would not be conducive because such type of selection of universe would be unmanageable. Hence, it is desired to have a proper sampling of the subordinate courts for heuristic study so that there appears to be proportionate representation of the whole universe. Obviously, two courts have represented each State, namely, one at the capital town and the other in the mufussil area. The selection of such representation has been on the basis of stratified systematic random sampling technique. Systematic random sampling technique is a variation of simple random sampling, which requires that the area and population can be uniquely identified by its order. By this technique of sampling respondents shall have an equal probability of being selected. The respondents in the area include the presiding officer of the courts, the Bar, the public (the litigants and non-litigants both), police organization, and the officials of the government, the law teachers and the law students. The researcher has taken care to collect data from the most remote areas of the country, viz., Leh Ladakh and Islands of Andaman and Nicobars in order to maximize the reliability as well as empirical generalizations.

(b) Data Collection

Data for the research study has been collected through both primary and secondary source; the tools for the selection of the primary data have been interview schedules (structured and unstructured), interview diary, and observation (participant and non-participant). In order to increase reliability of the interview schedules, these have been evaluated by six judges and pre-tested. The study of this type also falls heavily on the secondary source data and such data has been collected from different libraries of the country.

(c) Analysis

The data thus collected has been coded and tabulated in terms of dependents and independents variables in statistical tables. Wherever statistical analysis would not be possible the researcher would resort to descriptive analysis.

2

Profile of the Trial Court Judge

Socio-economic Educational Background

First and foremost, data regarding the socio-economic-educational background of the Trial Judges are presented. It is believed that the presentation of the background characteristic of the Trial Judges is *sine qua non* as the data on this parameter bear direct relation to need gratification and occupational attitudes of the Trial Judges adorning the Trial Judiciary which is an important independent impartial segment in the hierarchy of the judicial institutions that is conceived to dispense justice devoid of *Raga* (affection in favour of a party), *Lobha* (greed), *Bhaya* (fear), *Dvesha* (ill-will against a party), and *vadinoscha rahashrutihi* (the judge meeting and hearing a party to a case secretly). Justice is a sword which requires no scabbard. That perhaps seems to be the reason that our *Vedic Sutras, Nitikaras, Smritikaras,* and *Mimansakaras* prescribed the *Dharamdevata* (Goddess of Justice) the personification of Justice not as a blindfolded woman but an unfolded Goddess of Justice who is personified to be detached and impartial, unbiased and non-prejudicial; with open eyes she is personified not to be lured by *Raga, Lobha, Bhaya, Dvesha,* but open eyes permit the graceful rays flowing from its open eyes to illuminate justice. Goddess of Justice is also personified as *Dharamachakara* (wheel of Justice) which carries the entrenched inscription

Satyamevoddharamyaham and *Yato Dhrmastatojaya* which means Truth alone I uphold and where there is *Dharma* victory is there. This is the module of *Dharme Sarvam Pratishthtam*. This module of Justice, unlike western model, is presented the Goddess Justice either standing or seated in *Padamasana* on a throne clad with white shawl and raddish-yellow clothing (*Kashaya*) which exemplifies peace and purity and denotes renunciation. The Goddess Justice has four arms. On the right, one hand holds a scale which signifies to dispense justice equally, while the other lifts a sword signifying to punish severely in not upholding to *Dharma:* law; On the left, one hand holds the book of *Dharamsastra* (Law) in palms which signifies the offer of total knowledge of *Dharma:* Law to one and all equally, while the other lifts a whip which indicates to punish those who commit breach of *Dharma* : Law or those who defaced or defiled the command of *Dharma*: Law, viz., *Ne Vile Fano* (Do not defile the Temple of Justice).

In the backdrop of this keen glance of an eye of Justice and Goddess Justice, it is imperative to have a social audit of Trial Judges who have an intimate correlation with law, justice and profession. A close study of the background characteristics of Trial Judges may unfold many more aspects of the personality of Trial Judges who besides their vows: "What judgment shall I dread, doing no wrong";[1] "Judges like Caesar's wife should be above suspicion";[2] "Judges ought to be more learned than witty, more reverend than plausible, and more advised than confident".[3] The personality of Trial Judges should be above supercilious. The background characteristics of Trial Judges may be potent for predicting courtroom crafts and courtroom results, or may be relatively trivial predictive, or may be correlated with legal ability and may make a difference in courtroom results, or middle aged Trial Judges may seem to fare the best in court craft and

---

1. William Shakespeare (1564-1616), The Merchant of Venice, 1596-97, IV, i.
2. Bowen L.J. (1835-94), *Leeson* v. *General Council of Medical Education and Registration*, (1890), 43 Ch.D., 366 at 385.
3. Francis Bacon (1561-1626), Essays, 1625, LVI, *Of Judicature*.

court results, and less aged Trial Judges may seem to be less experienced in court craft and court results, and the older Trial Judges may possibly be fatigued one and may be slower in courtroom results. Quality education may be correlated with "Legal Justice Education" and may be potent to estimate legal ability to produce the unexpected courtroom craft as well as results, or may be potent to correlate with behavioural perspective, viz., on testing relations between their characteristics and their decision-making propensities. Background characteristics of Trial Judges include methods of recruitment, attitudes, political affiliations, etc.

TABLE 2.1

Sl. No.	Showing age of respondents	Response freq.	Response %age
1.	Up to 30 years	96	26.7
2.	30—40 years	126	35
3.	40—50 years	72	20
4.	50—60 years	66	18.3
	Total	360	100

The age group of these 360 Trial Judges of the Trial Judiciary starting from the difficult terrains of Leh Ladakh to the Islands of Andeman Nicobar range from 30 to 60 years. It has been found that the highest number of Trial Judges respondents are in the 30-40 (126:35%) years age group. 96:26.7% Trial Judges are below 30 years of age who might have joined afresh with little experience at the Bar, but preferred to join the Judiciary as Trial Judges at the early age with an eye to rise to the echelon. However, 72:20% and 66:18.3% are in the age group of 40-50 and 50-60 years and they are found in the senior positions at the Trial Judiciary, viz., Principal District Judges, Principal Sessions Judges, Senior Civil as well as Sessions Judges. Be that as it may, it is significant to submit that all the Trial Court Judges of the Subordinate Judiciary who gave interviews to the researcher were extremely cooperative and free, fair and fearless to share their experiences at the Courts right from the difficult terrains of Leh Ladakh to the Islands of Andeman Nicobar, from rural and urban areas, from cosmopolitan towns to Muffasils, and from remotest areas to the accessible areas of the places visited by the researchers in connection with this research project.

There are 98% males of Trial Judges-respondents, while 2% females are found in the law profession adorning the Bench. Hence, female respondents are less in presentation as compared to males. What could be the obvious and adequate reasons for the dearth of females in the Trial Judiciary need an in depth pointed studies. However, the researcher could not definitely ascertain any convincing reasons in this perspective.

TABLE 2.2

Sl. No.	*Religion of respondents*	*Response freq.*	*Response %age*
1.	Hindu	288	80
2.	Muslim	56	15
3.	Christian	06	1.7
4.	Parsi	10	2.8
5.	Any other	—	—
	Total	360	100

Tables 2.2 and 2.3 present the religion and caste background of the Trial Judges-respondents. 80% of the sample are Hindus and 15% are Muslims, 1.7% Christians and 2.8% are Parsis. The Hindus sample shows that Brahmins (132:36.6%) constitute the largest single group followed by the Kshatriyas (66:18.3%) and Vaishya (54:15%) that constitute the other group. The backward classes constitute 10% of the sample. Muslims sample shows that 8.4% are Sunni and 7.2% are Shia, whereas Christian sample demonstrates that 1.7% are Catholics.

The Trial Judges-respondents living within the municipal limits have urban background, and such respondents constitute a large sample (264:73.3%), while those

TABLE 2.3

Sl. No.	Showing Caste of respondents	Response freq.	Response %age
1.	Brahmin	132	36.6
2.	Kshatriya	66	18.3
3.	Vaishya	54	15
4.	SC/ST/OBC	36	10
5.	Sunni	30	8.4
6.	Shia	26	7.2
7.	Catholic	06	1.7
8.	Protestants	—	—
9.	Any other	10	2.8
	Total	360	100

TABLE 2.4

Sl. No.	Area of respondents	Response Frequency	Response %age
1.	Urban	264	73.3
2.	Rural	96	26.7
	Total	360	100

who have rural background, and such sample (96:26.7%) though less but does not represent the tiny as well as insignificant sample. There seems to be awakening amidst the rural populace, and as such liking for persuasion of higher learning in legal education. It may be further interesting to observe that the respondents with rural background seem to be desirous to participate in the developmental environment and human resource development through the annals of legal education.

The mother tongue of the Trial Judges-respondents as reflected in Table 2.5 is of the areas visited by the scholars within the temporal and financial restraints, viz., Jammu and Kashmir, Punjab, Haryana, Himachal Pradesh, Chandigarh, Delhi, Uttar Pradesh, Uttranchal, Madhya Pradesh, Rajasthan,

TABLE 2.5

Sl. No.	Mother Tongue of respondents	Response freq.	Response %age
1.	Marathi	120	32.96
2.	Bengali	24	6.59
3.	Hindi	30	8.24
4.	Punjabi	18	4.94
5.	Kashmiri	26	7.22
6.	Dogri	36	9.89
7.	Any other	30	8.24
8.	No response	76	20.87
	Total	360	98.95

Gujarat, Maharashtra, Goa, Kolkata, Andeman Nicobar, Madras, Cochin, Bangalore, Hyderabad. English language is common in all the places visited and used in Court process. Besides, Marathi is popular in Maharashtra and Goa, Bengali in Kolkata, Hindi in Hindi belt zones, whereas Konkani (Goa), Kanada (Bangolre), Malyalam (Cochin), Telgu (Hyderabad), Tamil (Madras), Urdu (J&K) languages fall under other category sample of the research project. Dogri and Kashmiri languages are widely spoken in the State of J&K.

TABLE 2.6

Sl. No.	Marital status of respondents	Response Frequency	Response %age
1.	Married	306	85
2.	Un—married	54	15
3	Divorcee/Widow/Widower	—	—
4.	Any other	—	—
	Total	360	100

306:85% Trial Judges-respondents are married, and 54:15% unmarried. Less percentage of response frequency shows that such Trial Judges are in quest of rehabilitation in the profession first and once they get settled they may then intend to have a happy married life that could culminate into professional satisfaction. The other inference could be drawn that such unmarried lawmen may not have the inkling towards marriage.

TABLE 2.7

Sl. No.	No. of dependants	Response freq.	Response %age
1.	One	12	3.3
2.	Two	42	11.7
3.	Three	24	6.7
4.	Four	42	11.7
5.	Five	36	10.0
6.	More than Five	30	8.3
7.	No Response	174	48.3
	Total	360	100

When the researcher examines the pattern with regard to the number of dependents (children, parents, unmarried brothers and sisters) these Trial Judges-respondents, the researcher finds that it varies to some extent according to their individual/personal situation. Table 2.7 shows these trends. The respondents who have wives, children, sisters, brothers and parents as dependents have twofold satisfaction, viz., completed their family procreation, and looking after their old aged parents as well as unsettled sisters and brothers as their *Dharama*. The unmarried respondents have their incomplete family, as they have not completed the stage of family procreation.

A succinct glance at the occupational position with educational level of the Trial Courts Judges-respondents shows that Munsiffs and District/Sessions Judges are equal in response-percentage frequency, while 6:1.60% are of the rank of Additional District Judges. Response frequency (12:3.33%) of Principal District Judges and Additional Sessions Judges (48:13.33%) has been encouraging and significant. Rest respondents-representatives are Sub-Judges, Chief Judicial

TABLE 2.8

Sl. No.	Present occupational status	Response freq.	Response %age
1.	Lawyer	06	1.6
2.	Munsiff	60	16.66
3.	Sub-Judge	54	15.00
4.	C.J.M.	18	05.00
5.	City Judge Junior Division	42	11.66
6.	City Judge Senior Division	36	10.00
7.	Sessions Judge/ Additional Sessions Judge/ 1st Additional Sessions Judge/ 2nd Additional Sessions Judge/ 3rd Additional Sessions Judge	48	13.33
8.	District and Sessions Judge	54	15.00
9.	Principal District Judge	12	03.33
10.	District Judge/ Additional District Judge/ 1st Additional District Judge/ 2nd Additional District Judge/ 3rd Additional District Judge	06	01.60
11.	Matrimonial Judge	—	—
12.	T.A.D.A. Court Judge	—	—
13.	Municipal Magistrate	—	—
14.	Any other	24	06.66
	Total	360	100

Magistrates, City Judge Junior Division and City Judge Senior Division.

The Trial Court Judges who have been gracious enough to respond to the research questionnaire are either two years LL.B. or three Years LL.B. degree holders from Pune, Bombay, Calcutta, Jammu, Kashmir, Punjab, H.P., G.N.D.U., Kurukshetra, Delhi, B.H.U., A.M.U., Panjabi, Lucknow, Allahabad, Goa, Madras, etc. Universities. Two Years LL.B. degree holders are pre-1966 stream of Legal Education and Three Years LL.B. degree holders are post-1966 stream of Legal Education. The researcher could not come in context any Trial Court Judge from Five Years stream of Legal Education. Insignificant respondents are Post Graduates (LL.M.) in Law.

TABLE 2.9

Sl. No.	Monthly Income of respondents	Response freq.	Response %age
1.	Up to Rs. 5000	—	—
2.	5001-10,000	18	5.00
3.	10,001-15,000	156	43.33
4.	15,001-20,000	78	21.66
5.	20,001-25,000	48	13.33
6.	25,000 and above	36	10.00
7.	No response	24	6.66
	Total	360	100

156:43.33% are in Rs.10,000-15,000 monthly income group, while 78:21.66% and 48:13.33% fall in Rs.15,000-20,000 and 20,000-25,000 respectively monthly income groups. 36:10.00% earn Rs. 25,000 and above per month. Majority of the Trial Court Judges have been benefited as per the recommendations of First National Judicial Commission Report (headed by Justice Jagannath Shetty).

TABLE 2.10

Sl. No.	Educational Qualification of parents	Response Freq. Father	Response Freq. Mother
1.	Illiterate	—	—
2.	Under Matric	06	12
3.	Matric	—	24
4.	Under-Graduate	12	18
5.	Graduate	24	42
6.	Post-Graduate	24	—
7.	Law-Graduate	54	—
8.	Technical & Ors.	06	—
	Total	126	96

Table 2.10 indicates the educational status of sociological parents—father and mother—of the Trial Judges-

respondents and that varies from illiteracy to adequate literacy to graduates to Post-graduates to Legal Baccalaurus to technical and professional education such as engineering/ medical, etc. It is interesting to note that majority of sociological fathers of the respondents are with legal background and that, perhaps, may be the influencing factor in making the respondents to adorn the Bench as Trial Judges.

TABLE 2.11

Sl. No.	Occupational Status of parents	Response Freq. Father	Response Freq. Mother
1.	Business	30	18
2.	Civil Services	36	—
3.	Defense Services	18	—
4.	Lawyer	54	—
5.	House Wife/un—employed	—	84
6.	Teaching	48	36
7.	Worker (skilled/unskilled)	—	—
8.	Judiciary	—	—
9.	Other	90	90
10.	No response	84	84
	Total	360	312

A scant look at Table 2.11 obviously makes it clear that the sociological parents—father and mother—of Trial Judges-respondents have diversification of profession/avocation. Interestingly, such responses reveal that majority belongs to Lawyers profession that may have ultimately influenced the respondents to choose legal profession. Other professions of sociological parents are business, civil service cadre, teaching (school, college and university) and defense service cadre. Agriculture, ministerial jobs, professional and technical jobs, etc. fall in 'other' category, and it may discern that such class too have the inclination that their wards pursuing higher education.

Income-wise break up of the sociological parents of the

TABLE 2.12

Sl. No.	Monthly Income of parents	Response Freq. Father	Response Freq. Mother	Response %age Father	Response % age Mother
1.	Upto Rs. 3000	—	24	—	6.66
2.	3001 – 4000	54	36	15.00	10.00
3.	4001—5000	18	12	05.00	03.30
4.	5001—6000	48	36	13.33	10.00
5.	6001—7000	12	24	03.33	06.66
6.	7001 & above	180	150	50.00	41.66
7.	No response	48	78	13.33	21.67
	Total	360	360	100	100

Trial Judges-respondents reveal that the majority are in the monthly income ranging between Rs. 7000 and above, 3000-4000 and 5000-6000.

TABLE 2.13

Sl. No.	Place of Practice	Response Frequency	Response %age
1.	Urban	240	66.66
2.	Rural	66	18.34
3.	No response	54	15.00
	Total	360	100

It was desired to know the place where did the respondents start practicing legal profession. Majority (240:66.66%) of the lawmen started practice at the Bar in the urban areas, and 66:18.34% preferred to practice in the rural areas of their origin in order to have deep insights into the working of law at the lowest/grass root level. However, none of the respondents had started practice of legal profession independently and they were attached with the senior counsels during their gestation period. Be that as it may, some of the respondents revealed that some seniors did take monetary care of juniors in the infancy stage of legal practice, but some of the respondents did not hesitate to unfold the pangs of being treated as bonded labour for years together by their seniors as such seniors did not care to look after the pocket money of their juniors.

TABLE 2.14

Sl. No.	Political affiliations of respondents	Response Freq.	Response %age
1.	Indian National Congress	96	26.67
2.	Bhartiya Janata Party	72	20.00
3.	C.P.I.	—	—
4.	C.P.M.	—	—
5.	Samta Party	—	—
6.	J.D.	—	—
7.	Local Regional Party	06	01.66
8.	No response	186	51.67
	Total	360	100

Tables 2.14 and 2.15 reflect the responses of the respondents as to their political affiliations and continuous political ideologue affinity. Majority have had political affiliations either with Indian National Congress (96:26.67%) or Bhartiya Janata Party (72:20.00%). However, insignificant percentage 6:01.66% keep their political affiliations with local regional political parties. Majority 186:51.67% who did not respond to the query may have some hesitation to disclose

TABLE 2.15

Sl. No.	Whether same political ideology observed	Response Frequency	Response %age
1.	Yes	138	38.33
2.	No	78	21.67
3.	No response	144	40.00
	Total	360	100

their political affiliations, but during the discussion at the time of interview they too have some political affiliations but afraid to give vent to.

It is interesting as well as intriguing to note from the responses that the respondents with political affiliations continue to observe political ideologue. Whether such political ideologies carry impetus on their professional output though may be a million dollars question, but it is nevertheless an interesting revelation of the judicial history that 'transcendental meditation' and 'Gandhian philosophy' did mark indelible impetus on professional output.

TABLE 2.16

Sl. No.	*Whether parents observe same political ideology*	*Response Frequency*	*Response %age*
1.	Yes	150	41.67
2.	No	60	16.66
3.	No response	150	41.67
	Total	360	100

And, similar are the political affiliations as well as political ideologue of the sociological parents of the respondents, and this what is revealing from the close scrutiny of the statistics presented in Table 2.16. It is expedient to present that sociological parents' political ideologue do carry impetus on the respondents to follow political ideologue affinity of their sociological parents in order to carry forward family traditions.

The statistical data presented in Tables 2.17 and 2.18 unfold the responses of the respondents relating to the methods/mechanisms of recruitment/selection/appointment as Trial Judges of Trial Courts in different States of Union of India that is *Bharat*. Figures speak for self.

Though now there is no prerequisite of practice experience at the Bar to be eligible for recruitment as a Trial Judge at the Trial Court, but it used to be imperative to have

TABLE 2.17

Sl. No.	Recruitment Method/ Agency	Response Frequency	Response %age
1.	State Public Service Commission	180	50.00
2.	Selection Board constituted by State High Court	42	11.67
3.	Selection Board constituted by State Government	36	10.00
4.	Any other	12	03.33
5.	No response	90	25.00
	Total	360	100

TABLE 2.18

Sl. No.	Appointing authority	Response Frequency	Response %age
1.	State Governor	276	76.67
2.	Chief Justice of High Court	36	10.00
3.	Any other	—	—
4.	No response	48	13.33
	Total	360	100

TABLE 2.19

Sl. No.	Actual practice	Response Frequency	Response %age
1.	One year	—	—
2.	Two Years	—	—
3.	Three years	216	60.00
4.	Four years	60	16.67
5.	Five years & above	30	08.33
6.	No response	54	15.00
	Total	360	100

minimum practice experience at the Bar to be eligible to compete for Trial Judge for the Trial Judiciary. The Trial Judges-respondents either have had three years (216:60.00%) or four years (60:16.67%) or five and above years (30:8.33%) experience at the Bar before being selected/appointed as Trial Judges of the Trial Courts.

TABLE 2.20

Sl. No.	Recruitment Quota	Response Frequency	Response %age
1.	Direct Recruitment	144	40.00
2.	Open Merit	126	35.00
3.	Selection from the members of Bar	60	16.67
4.	Selection from members of S.C/S.T/O.B.C.	30	08.33
	Total	360	100

Table 2.20 is revealing with regard to recruitment quota policy, such as selection/appointment under open merit (126:35.00%), constitutionally permissible compatible reserved categories, viz., S.C./S.T./O.B.C. (30:08.33%), direct recruitment, viz., in service promotion to upper stratum (144:40%), and direct selection/appointment from the members of Bar, viz., direct appointment as District/Sessions Judge with minimum Bar experience of ten years (60:16.67%).

TABLE 2.21

Sl. No.	Method of recruitment	Response Frequency	Response %age
1.	Written Exams	24	06.67
2.	Oral Viva—voce	12	03.33
3.	Both	216	60.00
4.	No response	108	30.00
	Total	360	100

The Trial Court Judges have had to qualify both written and oral examinations in the competitions duly conducted by appropriate bodies, and that what Table 2.21 is about.

TABLE 2.22

Sl. No.	*Language during recruitment*	*Response Frequency*	*Response %age*
1.	Yes	252	70.00
2.	No	12	03.33
3.	No response	96	26.67
	Total	360	100

Language in competing for Trial Court Judges is primarily English or Hindi or other local/State languages recognized by the Constitution of India, viz., Urdu, Tamil, Telgu, Marathi, Gujarati, Bangala, etc. This is the language of responses recorded in Table 2.22.

TABLE 2.23

Sl. No.	*Emergency Recruitment*	*Response Frequency*	*Response %age*
1.	Yes	114	31.67
2.	No	48	13.33
3.	No response	198	55.00
	Total	360	100

There may be urgent/emergency occasions to recruit/ appoint Trial Judges for the trial of special/emergency cases, and as such the respondents were probed to record their impressions to this variable, and the statistical figures recorded in Table 2.23 speak about such emergency recruitment situations.

The impressions relating to minimum educational qualifications for selection/appointment/recruitment as Trial

TABLE 2.24

Sl. No.	Minimum Educational Qualifications	Response Frequency	Response %age
1.	LL.B.	276	76.67
2.	Any other	—	—
3.	No response	84	23.33
	Total	360	100

Court Judges have been presented in Table 2.24 and the majority 276:76.67% respondents responded that LL.B. (3 years or 5 years) is the minimum statutory qualification for selection/appointment/recruitment as Trial Court Judges. 84:23.33% did respond to this variable for the reasons best known to such respondents.

TABLE 2.25

Sl. No.	Disqualification	Response Frequency	Response %age
1.	Bigamy	—	—
2.	Conviction	30	08.33
3.	Misconduct	42	11.67
4.	All the above	222	66.67
5.	Any other	—	—
6.	No response	66	18.33
	Total	360	100

Bigamy, conviction, misconduct are the statutory disqualifications for selection/appointment as Trial Court Judges.

High Court(s), State Public Service Commission(s), State Government(s), State Judicial Services Commission(s) are the recognized recruiting agencies for selection/appointment of Trial Court Judges, and the statistical data, as per responses of the respondents, on this variable is recorded in Table 2.26.

Table 2.27 indicates the nature of members of

TABLE 2.26

Sl. No.	Recruitment Agency	Response Frequency	Response %age
1.	High Court	30	08.33
2.	State Public Service Commission	120	33.33
3.	State Government	108	30.00
4.	State Judicial Services	30	08.33
5.	No response	72	20.00
	Total	360	100

TABLE 2.27

Sl. No.	Members of recruitment Board	Response Frequency	Response %age
1.	Chief Justice of High Court or a Judge of High Court deputed by the Chief Justice	174	48.33
2.	Two Judges of the High Court nominated by the Chief—Justice	108	30.00
3.	Chief Secretary of the State	12	03.33
4.	Law Secretary nominated by Governor	—	—
5.	Committee of Judges constituted by Chief Justice	—	—
6.	Any other	—	—
7.	No response	66	18.33
	Total	360	100

recruitment board for the selection/appointment of Trial Court Judges, and in majority cases either the Chief Justice of the State High Court or his nominee(s) (174:48.33%, 108:30%) form the components of recruitment boards/agencies for the selection/appointment of Trial Judges of Trial Courts and the presence of Higher Judges ascertain the maximum proximity of selection/appointment of righteous persons as Trial Judges of Trial Courts who ultimately are deemed to be responsible to retain, sustain, conserve, observe, preserve the dignity as well as independence of the Trial Judiciary.

TABLE 2.28

Sl. No.	Experience as Trial Court Judge	Response Frequency	Response %age
1.	Up to 5 years	60	16.67
2.	5—10 years	120	33.33
3.	10—15 years	24	06.66
4.	15—20 years	18	05.00
5.	20—25 years	36	10.00
6.	25—30 years	12	03.33
7.	No response	90	25.00
	Total	360	100

Table 2.28 tell about the judicial experience of Trial Court Judges as Trial Court Judges ranging from the lowest stratum Munsif to highest stratum District/Sessions Judge. Responses relating to experience as Trial Court Judges vary according to stratum-position. Respondents with experience between 5-10 years (120:33.33%), 20-25 years (36:10.00%) 10-15 years (24:6.66%) and up to 5 years (60:16.67%) were responsive to the variables, while respondents of high stratum at District/Sessions level were conservative in responding to variables, and as such their experience responses range between 25-30 years (12:3.33%).

TABLE 2.29

Sl. No.	Promotional expectancy	Response Frequency	Response %age
1.	Yes	324	90.00
2.	No	36	10.00
3.	No response	—	—
	Total	360	100

Tables 2.29 and 2.30 reflect the responses of the Trial Court Judges-respondents as to Promotional expectancy during service tenure from minimum stratum to highest stratum as Trial Judges and the criterion followed/adapted in

TABLE 2.30

Sl. No.	Promotional selection criteria	Response Frequency	Response %age
1.	Merit	300	
2.	Caste/Community/ Regional Identification	—	
3.	Political affiliation	—	
4.	Any other	—	
5.	No response	24	
	Total	324	

promotional selections. Every Trial Judge has have the expectancy to rise to the highest as Trial Court Judge at the Subordinate Courts. There is a specious complaint/allegation that promotional selections are generally made with political recommendations, but the responses unfold the mist that merit alone plays predominant role in promotional selections. Political interferences/recommendations are part of the system in a democracy country like India, and judicial institution may not be untouched from this calamity, but that is not as alarming as it is speciously projected to be. For this reason alone judicial institution is known as the least dangerous branch of the government, least dangerous than the executive and the legislature.

TABLE 2.31

Sl. No.	Pre/post retirement position expected	Response Frequency	Response %age
1.	Elevation to High Court	234	65.00
2.	Any other	18	05.00
3.	No response	108	30.00
	Total	360	100

It is interesting to note that majority of respondents 234:65% have the inclination/desire while in active service to get elevation as a High Court Judge in the respective state, while a minority respondents 18:05% too have the inclination to get some post-retirement position.

TABLE 2.32

Sl. No.	Trial Courts in respondent's state	Response Frequency	Response %age
1.	High Court	—	—
2.	Trial Courts (Subordinate courts)	—	—
3.	Principal District and Sessions Judge	—	—
4.	Additional District and Sessions Judge	—	—
5.	Senior Subordinate Judge	—	—
6.	Junior Sub-Judge	—	—
7.	2-7 trial courts structure	318	88.33
8.	No response	42	11.67
	Total	360	100

The Trial Courts Judges-respondents were probed to respond to reflect their responses relating to the nature/ structure of Trial Courts in their respective State, and in almost majority of them 318:88.33% responded the nature of Trial Courts structure beginning from lowest stratum Munsiff to highest stratum Principal District/Sessions Judge in their respective State. However, 42:11.67% have not responded to the variable.

TABLE 2.33

Sl. No.	Distance between residence and Trial Court	Response Frequency	Response %age
1.	Less than 1 k.m.	48	13.33
2.	1-2 kms.	54	15.00
3.	2-4 kms.	48	13.33
4.	4-6 kms.	48	13.33
5.	More than 6 kms.	96	26.67
6.	No response	66	18.34
	Total	360	100

The statistical figures present the distance between residence and Trial Courts of Trial Courts Judges-respondents. 96:26.67% have to travel more than 6 kms. a day to the place of work-destination and similar distance for backward travel; 48:13.33%, 48:13.33% have to travel between 4-6 kms. and 2-4 kms. respectively from residence to work-destination and with similar distance to back home; 54:15% travel between 1-2 kms. from their residence to work-destination place and with similar distance from work-destination place to home; 48:13.33% travel less than 1 km. a day between residence to work-destination place. The nature of this type of responses present time consumed in travel and its impetus on working capacity, i.e. whether keeping the Trial Judge relaxed or fatigued, and ultimately impetus on output result. Could this be presumed as one of the causes for the occurrence of delay in the disposal of cases is a million dollar question to be penetrated in depth?

TABLE 2.34

Sl. No.	*Means of Transport*	*Response frequency*	*Response percentage*
1.	Own Scooter	30	8.33
2.	Own Car	66	18.33
3.	Official Car	192	53.33
4.	Pool Car	18	05.00
5.	Public transport	12	3.34
6.	Taxi /Auto Rickshaw	—	—
7.	On Foot	42	11.67
	Total	360	100

It is interesting to note that majority use official car (192:53.33%) as means of transportation, while 18:05% use pool car for transportation. 66:18.33% use own car and 30:8.33% own scooters and as such use it as means of transportation, while 42:11.67% significantly move on foot from their home to the working place-destination. Public transport is another mode of transport, which plies on the roads of different States in plenty, and 12:3.34% use it as a means of transportation to reach their destination.

3

Attitude and Aptitude to be a Trial Court Judge

Attitude and aptitude are behaviouralists approach to the human mind in general, and more particularly to the judicial mind of a lower (Trial) court judge. As a lower (Trial) court judge, he decides cases in accordance with what he finds the law to be, and rarely or occasionally he may make clear what he thinks it ought be. Succinctly, behavioural study is a psychometric study of Trial Judges that examines their "minds", their "attitudes", their "aptitudes" to be Judges to adorn the trial judiciary who may, presumably, have the values that play significantly in the jurisprudence of a Kane, a Holmes, a Halsbury, a Julius Stone, a Roscoe Pound, a Cardozo, a Patanjali Shastri, a Gajendragadkar, a Hydayyatulla, a Subbarao, a Krishna Iyer, a Bhagwati, etc., etc. to mention a few Justices heroes!

Indisputably, ii is agreed that attitude and aptitude inhere at the indispensable function of human organization, and are instinct dwelling in every being. It may not be utopian to say that without attitude and aptitude a person may be insensitive or non-social animal.[1] The concept of

1. See, The Neo-Behavioural Approach to the Judicial Process: A Critique, in Wallace Mendelson, Supreme Court Statecraft, 1987, 265.

attitude and aptitude are by and large psychological which "relate to those forces operating within the individual ... which impel certain ways"[2] and are the basic elements of all human behaviour, and are related to some kind of mental activity. Attitudes and aptitudes have also relationship with motivation, temperaments, likes, dislikes and idiosyncrasies having impetus in the decision-making process.

In the backdrop of the above, the data on the theme may be helpful to understanding the "belief that human motivations include some inborn factors"[3] relating to the dimensions of attitudes and aptitudes of Trial Judges. A scientific attitude and aptitude means, says Francis Galton, "an inherent stimulus to climb the path that leads to knowledge with the strength to reach the summit."[4] In the total fabric of norms, ideology, behaviouralism, attitudes are not susceptible to legal treatment.[5]

In the backdrop of the above, the data on the theme unfold the mists of attitudes and aptitudes of Trial Judges.

TABLE 3.1

Sl. No.	*Duration of LL.B. Degree*	*Response Frequency*	*Response percentage*
1.	Two years	—	—
2.	Three Years	144	40.00
3.	Five years	—	—
4.	No Response	216	60.00
	Total	360	100

In Table 3.1 the responses of the Trial Court Judges have been recorded relating to the nature of Law Degree they have obtained before joining the legal profession, and in

2. See Harold Koontz, et.al., Essentials of Management, 1982
3. See Julius Stone, Social Dimensions of Law and Justice, 1999, 488.
4. See P.V. Young, Scientific Social Surveys and Research, 1977, p.123.
5. See Robert Bierstedt, The Social Order, 1970, p. 478.

majority 144:40% the respondents are Law Graduates of 3 years duration course commencing in 1966 with the launch of new education policy. However, none of the respondents seem to be from 5 years LL.B. stream that started in 1986 with the opening of National Law School of India University at Bangalore, the first Law University not only in India but in the whole of the world, and the product from NLSUI prefers to join legal firms/MNCs/Solicitors firms than joining Judiciary at the low ebb. 216:60% respondents who did not respond to the query, however, seem to be from 2 years LL.B. stream—a pre-1966 legal education stream.

TABLE 3.2

Sl. No.	*University Granting LL.B. Degree*	*Response Frequency*	*Response percentage*
1.	Calcutta	24	06.66
2.	Bombay	42	11.66
3.	Poona	90	25.00
4.	Jammu	18	05.00
5.	Kashmir	24	06.66
6.	Others	102	28.33
	Total	360	100

The statistical figures presented in Table 3.2 show varying responses relating to the University where from the Trial Court Judges-respondents have obtained their Law Degrees. Others include Delhi, Universities in Uttar Pradesh, Madhya Pradesh, Rajasthan, Gujarat, Panjab, Haryana, Himachal Pradesh, etc.

In majority 216:60%, the Trial Court Judges-respondents have been successful in obtaining Law Degree with second division. However, 60:16.66% respondents have had brilliant academic record with first division. It may be inferred that the respondents joining the judiciary have average or above average academic record.

TABLE 3.3

Sl. No.	Division secured in LL.B.	Response Frequency	Response percentage
1.	I Division	60	16.66
2.	II Division	216	60.00
3.	III Division	—	—
4.	No Response	84	23.34
	Total	360	100

TABLE 3.4

Sl. No.	Persuasion of LL.M. Studies	Response Frequency	Response percentage
1.	Yes	24	06.67
2.	No	312	86.66
3.	No Comment	24	06.67
	Total	360	100

The statistics recorded in Table 3.4 show that insignificant number of Trial Court Judges-respondents 24:06.67% have pursued LL.M. degree and majority respondents 312:86.66% have satisfaction with LL.B. degree only, and as such they have no inclination to have higher degrees in legal education of *legum magistare.*

TABLE 3.5

Sl. No.	Persuasion of Doctorate in law	Response Frequency	Response percentage
1.	Yes	12	03.33
2.	No	348	96.67
3.	No Comment	—	—
	Total	360	100

Similarly, half of the *legum magistare* respondents 12:3.33% have had pursued Doctorate Degree in Law and the majority 348:96.67% have no inclination towards higher legal education degrees.

TABLE 3.6

Sl. No.	*Practice Experience at Pre-Judgeship level*	*Response Frequency*	*Response Percentage*
1.	Up to Five years	66	18.33
2.	Five to Ten years	138	38.33
3.	Ten to Fifteen years	30	08.34
4.	Fifteen years and above	—	—
5.	No response	126	35.00
	Total	360	100

Table 3.6 reflects the responses relating to the variable pre-judgeship professional practice experiences of the Trial Court Judges-respondents that varies from five years (66:18.33%) to five to ten years (138:38.33%), and ten to fifteen years (30:8.34%). However, significant percentage of the respondents 126:35% did not like to part with the information relating to the above stated variable, but, nevertheless, such respondents could not be escapee from the varying professional practice experiences as indicated above.

TABLE 3.7

Sl. No.	*Intention to become Lawyer*	*Response Frequency*	*Response Percentage*
1.	Yes	282	78.34
2.	No	24	06.66
3.	Can't say	54	15.00
	Total	360	100

Majority Trial Court Judges-respondents 282:78.34% have aptitude, attitude and self-motivation to be Lawyers and as such they have pursued legal education as a career.

Motivational factors have intimate correlation in pursuit of knowledge in legal education and striving for becoming a lawyer, or looking for some other occupation avocations with legal education as a background. Motivation is a process through which an individual strives towards accomplishment of a cherished or desired career-objective. He cannot accomplish it unless and until he knows what motivates him to accomplish it. Problems of motivation are complex on the one hand, and important on the other hand in the arena of legal science. However, minority of the respondents 24:06.66% seem to have drifted towards this profession, and though they seem to have no urges, drives, desires, aspirations, strivings for this noble profession, but the needs of human beings compulsions, viz., economic, may have been the methodological impediments for behaviour drift—psychological, societal, economic, familial—towards this noble profession. Needless to say, need is the basis of behaviour change. However, 54:15% respondents have nothing to spell out and as such they may seem to be oscillating between natural attitude/aptitude/motivation human instinct and drifted human behaviour pattern.

TABLE 3.8

Sl. No.	*Intention to become Judge*	*Response Frequency*	*Response Percentage*
1.	During studentship	84	23.34
2.	During Practice	66	18.33
3.	Both	144	40.00
4.	No Comment	66	18.34
	Total	360	100

Similarly, 84:23.34% have had the aptitude/attitude/motivation/urge/drives/aspirations/strivings to be a Judge at the Trial level as a career during the days of studentship while pursuing legal education; 66:18.33% have had it during gestation period of initial practice, while 144:40% have had it at both the levels, i.e. during studentship as well as during internship practice. 66:18.34% did not respond to the variable and as such they seem to be drifted towards it for the similar reasons explained in the preceding Table.

TABLE 3.9

Sl. No.	Decision as to legal career	Response Frequency	Response Percentage
1.	You yourself	162	49.09
2.	Your parents	150	45.45
3.	Friends (Law/Non—Law)	18	05.45
4.	Teacher	—	—
5.	No response	30	08.34
	Total	360	100

The Trial Court Judges-respondents were asked specifically to record their impressions to the variable as to who has been decision-making factor to choosing legal profession as a legal career for them. 162:49.09% have taken up legal career out of their own desire, 150:45.45% said that they did so in deference to the wishes of their parents or family's wishes as they were responsible to moulding them to take up legal career for becoming more articulate, 18:5.45% did feel open to share that their friends—some law and some non-law—have had been instrument to take a decision to take up legal career for becoming more articulate, and those who did not respond 30:8.34% seem to be drifted toward law to take it up as a career.

TABLE 3.10

Sl. No.	Order of choice	Response Frequency	Response Percentage
1.	First Choice	294	81.66
2.	Second Choice	24	06.66
3.	Third Choice	12	03.33
4.	No Comment	30	08.33
	Total	360	100

The statistical data in this Table demonstrate that the varied circumstances contribute to adapt a perceptive vision to developing the aptitude for legal career. As a legal career whether the legal profession, i.e. presiding officer of the Trial Court, has been a first or second choice for them, and the responses presented tell varied stories, irrespective of motivational correlations, viz., 294:81.66% have had their first choice to be presiding officers of Trial Courts, while 24:06.66% and 12:03.33% have had second and third choice respectively to be presiding officers of Trial Courts. Those who have not responded seem to be drifted towards legal career for the identical reasons recorded in the preceding Tables.

TABLE 3.11

Sl. No.	Any family member in legal profession	Response Frequency	Response Percentage
1.	Yes	204	56.66
2.	No	138	38.34
3.	No Comment	18	05.00
	Total	360	100

The Trial Court Judges-respondents who have had chosen legal profession as legal career either of their own choice, or the choice of their parents, or the choice of their law/non-law friends, or drifted, 204:56.66% have had family members in legal profession, while 138:38.34% have had no family members in this noble legal profession.

And, such respondents whose family members have been in the legal profession, were further probed to give vent to their free, frank, and fair feelings whether such family members in the legal profession have had been, in any way, a source of inspiration for them, i.e. moulding or reshaping the motivational attitude/aptitude to take up legal career?

The responses to such probing have been presented in this Table 3.12, and the statistical figures are self explanatory, viz., 222:61.66% have replied in the affirmative, while 66:18.33% have answered in the negative.

TABLE 3.12

Sl. No.	As to source of inspiration	Response Frequency	Response Percentage
1.	Yes	222	61.66
2.	No	66	18.33
3.	No Comment	72	20.00
	Total	360	100

TABLE 3.13

Sl. No.	Consideration of other alternatives in career	Response Frequency	Response Percentage
1.	Yes	138	38.34
2.	No	192	53.33
3.	No Comment	30	08.33
	Total	360	100

The Trial Court Judges-respondents interviewed for the present research study who have had opted for legal career for one reason or the other as explained above, were further interviewed to pen down their concern whether did they consider other alternatives of their career, besides legal career, and 138:38.34% such lawmen did mention unhesitatingly that they did consider other alternatives as their career besides the legal profession. However, 192:53.33% did not consider any other alternatives as their career except the legal profession as career. What other alternatives as would be career did they chose? The interviewees' responses to this variable have been exhibited in Table 3.14.

It seems from the data presented in Table 3.14 that Engineering 42:30.44%, Medical 18:13.04%, Defense services 18:13.04% continue to haunt persons to opt for either of these professions as careers, while to be either scientists 18:13.04% or bureaucrats 12:08.68% or teachers 6:04.34% or other lucrative jobs/ministerial jobs 24:17.39% have been the other alternative careers options with the respondents.

TABLE 3.14

Sl. No.	Alternative career opted	Response Frequency	Response Percentage
1.	Doctor	18	13.04
2.	Engineer	42	30.44
3.	Scientist	18	13.04
4.	Banking Service	0	00.00
5.	School/College/University Teacher	6	04.34
6.	I.A.S./I.P.S./I.F.S. etc.	12	08.68
7.	Defence Services	18	13.04
8.	Labour Welfare Officer	—	—
9.	Other services	24	17.39
	Total	138	100

The lawmen that once thought to have had some alternatives for their careers were asked pointedly that in case they decided on an alternative career for themselves then why did they choose legal career for them.

TABLE 3.15

Sl. No.	Competition for other competitive examinations	Response Frequency	Response Percentage
1.	Yes	48	13.34
2.	No	144	40.00
3.	No Comment	168	46.66
	Total	360	100

TABLE 3.16

Sl. No.	Passing of written paper in competitive examinations	Response Frequency	Response Percentage
1.	Yes	60	16.66
2.	No	108	30.00
3.	No Comment	192	53.34
	Total	360	100

Such respondents did mention that they did compete for competition examinations and somehow did succeed or failed to succeed either in IAS/IPS/IFS/State Administrative Services/State Public Services/Banking/Defense Services/etc. and could not come up in the final list of selected candidates for appointment and as such did not pursue the alternatives careers and opted Trial Court Presiding Officers as legal careers.

4

Job Satisfaction and Infrastructure Facilities

Job satisfaction largely depends on the availability of infrastructure facilities at the working place, which ultimately culminate into efficiency in the decision-making process. As such, in this part an endeavour has been made to present the data concerning the tenets of infrastructure facilities. The collection of data on this parameter was *sine qua non* in order to establish correlations between the job satisfaction and the trends of efficiency in the job output which is no doctrinaire treatment but which stands close to actual life.

TABLE 4.1

Sl. No.	*Job satisfaction as a Judge*	*Response Frequency*	*Response Percentage*
1.	Yes	306	85.00
2.	No	36	10.00
3.	No Comment	18	05.00
	Total	360	100

In Table 4.1 the impressions of Trial Court Judges relating to job satisfaction as well as security as a Trial Court Judge have been recorded. Cut of the sample of 360, 306:85%

respondents have meaningful job satisfaction as a Trial Court Judge, while 36:10% only feel dissatisfied. However, 18:05% did not prefer to respond or comment as to their satisfaction or dissatisfaction to the job as a Trial Court Judge and it may infer that such category of Trial Judges may either is casual to the profession or indifferent to the profession or mock to the profession.

TABLE 4.2

Sl. No.	*Type of Accommodation availed*	*Response Frequency*	*Response Percentage*
1.	Own House	90	25.00
2.	Rented accommodation	108	30.00
3.	Govt. Accommodation	120	33.34
4.	Any other	12	03.33
5.	No Comment	30	08.33
	Total	360	100

Table 4.2 presents the responses as to the type of accommodation the Trial Court Judges live in. Majority 120:33.34% live in government provided accommodation according to their status/position, 108:30% live in rented accommodation either because of non-availability of government accommodation or preferring to avail house rent facilities and live in hired/rented accommodation of the rent of their own choice, 90:25% live in their houses either self acquired or succession acquired or in-laws gift.

TABLE 4.3

Sl. No.	*Availing of L.T.C. / Home Town facility*	*Response Frequency*	*Response Percentage*
1.	Yes	126	35.00
2.	No	162	45.00
3.	No Comment	72	20.00
	Total	360	100

Availing of L.T.C./Home Town L.T.C. facility is one of the contributing factors of job satisfaction, and as such the respondents were pointedly probed to record their impressions on this variable. Table 4.3 presents the statistics in this perspective. Majority 162:45% have had no occasion to avail this facility, 126:35% have had the occasion to avail this facility, 72:20% have no comments or response to make.

TABLE 4.4

Sl. No.	*Frequency of making use of the facility*	*Response Frequency*	*Response Percentage*
1.	Very frequent	—	—
2.	Frequent	—	—
3.	Occasional	102	28.34
4.	Rarely	36	10.00
5.	No response	222	61.66
	Total	360	100

The responses relating to the frequency of making use of L.T.C./Home Town L.T.C. have been presented in Table 4.4. 102:28.34% make occasional use of this facility, 36:10% take advantage of this facility rarely, 222:61.66% have not responded to the variable.

TABLE 4.5

Sl. No.	*Medical Facility availed*	*Response Frequency*	*Response Percentage*
1.	Self	138	38.33
2.	Family	156	43.34
3.	Dependent	66	18.33
	Total	360	100

The governments both at the Center and States have prescribed some kind of medical facilities to their employees in one form or the other either indoor treatment or outdoor treatment or medical reimbursement or medico-claim insurance, and the lawmen were pointedly asked to respond to the variable whether they ever take advantage of this facility. Responses show that they do take advantage of medical facility in whichever form available either for self (138:38.33%), or for their family (156:43.34%), or for their dependents who have been declared to be dependents in their official records (66:18.33%). The frequency of availing the medical facility may vary or depend upon the nature of emergency as well as eventuality, and as such its claim may sometimes be "very frequently" or "frequently" or "occasionally" or "rarely".

TABLE 4.6

Sl. No.	*Limit to Medical Facility*	*Response Frequency*	*Response Percentage*
1.	Yes	168	46.66
2.	No	42	11.07
3.	No Comment	150	41.67
	Total	360	100

"Whether such medical facility is with certain limit", the responses to this variable have been presented in Table 4.6, and the majority 168:46.66% have expressed in affirmative, while 42:11.07% have expressed otherwise, and a quite significant number of respondents 150:41.67% have not been in a position to articulate any comments. Quite surprising!

TABLE 4.7

Sl. No.	*Type of Limitation*	*Response Frequency*	*Response Percentage*
1.	Specification as to Doctor	150	89.28
2.	Monitory limit	—	—
3.	Fixed Medical reimbursement	18	10.72
4.	No response	—	—
	Total	168	100

Those who have expressed that the medical facility is made use of with certain limits were further pointedly asked to respond to "What sorts of the limitations is imposed"? From the statistics presented in Table 4.7 it is evident that medical facility is available with two types of limitations, viz., specification as to Doctor/medical practitioner (150:89.28%) and fixed medical reimbursement (18:10.72%).

TABLE 4.8

Sl. No.	*Availability of other facilities*	*Response Frequency (as to Govt. facility)*	*Response Frequency (as to self facility)*
1.	Telephone facility	180	126
2.	Computer	—	114
3.	Fax	114	60
4.	Electronic/Manual Typewriter	114	120
5.	Law Library	114	180
	Total	522	600

The efficiency in work out put depends upon the nature of physical/infrastructure facilities made available to the Trial Court Judges both in the Trial Courts as well as at home either at government expenses or at self expenses. Facilities in the form of telephone, computer, fax, electronic typewriter, manual typewriter, law library are made available to the Trial Court Judges in the Trial Courts at government expenses, and the similar types of facilities the Trial Court Judges these days keep at their homes at their own expenses.

In order to increase efficiency in court work out put it is *sine qua non* on the government to provide modern electronic facilities to the Trial Court Judges at the Trial Courts and the Trial Courts, as per Justice Shetty Commission Report, have been provided with computer, etc. facilities. However, computers should not be used as sophisticated typewriters for court work output, but they must be utilized to the optimum with regard to internet, intra and inter linkage, connections with Higher Courts, E-conferencing, etc.

TABLE 4.9

Sl. No.	Availability of other facilities in Court	Response Frequency (as to Govt. facility)
1.	Telephone facility	342
2.	Computer	210
3.	Fax	342
4.	Electronic/Manual Typewriter	342
5.	Law Library	342
	Total	1578

in order to have quick disposal of cases to unloading the Trial Courts with loaded cases in millions. Be that as it may, in some places visited by the researcher it has been observed that the computers have been kept unattended to thus making way for the dust to pile on computers, or due to dearth of computer trained personnel the computers have been kept unused in most of the Trial Courts in the country. However, it has been interesting to note that in Pune, Bombay, Andeman and Nicobar the Trial Courts have been well equipped with the computers with optimum as well as excellent use. Though computers have been provided in the most difficult terrain area of Leh and Ladakh but kept unused.

TABLE 4.10

Sl. No.	Availability of adequate staff	Response Frequency	Response percentage
1.	Steno	312	86.66
2.	Reader	312	86.66
3.	Clerk	312	86.66
4.	Case Teller	312	86.66
5.	Peon	312	86.66
6	Nazir	312	86.66
7.	Pyada	312	86.66
8.	Process Server	312	86.66
9.	No response	48	13:34

Except few, in almost all the Trial Court Judges-respondents have fairly responded that adequate staff has been made available to them in court process in the nature of steno, reader, clerk, case teller, peon, *nazir*, *payada*, process server, case caller.

TABLE 4.11

Sl. No.	Generalist approach as basic cause of delay	Response Frequency	Response Percentage
1.	Yes	228	63.34
2.	No	114	31.66
3.	No Comment	18	05.00
	Total	360	100

The presiding officers of the Trial Courts have been assigned varied nature of civil, criminal, family/matrimonial, anti-corruption, rent, municipal, excise, electricity, forest, traffic, bank TADA/POTA, land disputes, cinematography, registration, motor accident claims, etc. cases under different laws as the nature of the case may be. The presiding officers of the Trial Courts develop one mind set in the disposal of cases, and once they are transferred to handle another nature of cases it consumes some time to shift to another mind trend setting. Sometimes the same presiding officer has to decide different nature of cases thus becoming a generalist Judge of the Trial Court instead an expertise. And in this process, it is the general feeling that the generalist approach to the disposal of cases is the basic cause of delay, because the application of the mind of the Trial Judge from one trend setting to another trend setting consumes time. The respondents in majority 228:63.34% have agreed with this variable, whereas 114:31.66% have expressed disagreement with this variable, while 18:05% have no comments to offer.

It is *sine qua non* to know in depth the causal factors for causing delay in the disposal of cases at the Trial Court level. It is not one cause but multiplicity of causes as the roots for delay in the disposal of cases. It is difficult to pin point towards a particular cause for delay. Therefore, it has

TABLE 4.12

Sl. No.	Cause of delay	Response Frequency	Response Percentage
1.	Due to Judges	12	03.33
2.	Due to Advocates	48	13.34
3.	Due to Litigant	54	15.00
4.	Due to Legal Procedures	—	—
5.	All the above	228	63.33
6.	Any other	—	—
7.	No comment	18	05.00
	Total	360	100

rightly been observed that delay is a riddle wrapped in mystery inside an enigma. Delay may be due to attitudinal approaches of Judges, Advocates, Litigants and niceties as well as interstices with legal procedures, this what is the majority response 228:63.33% of the Trial Court Judges-respondents themselves. How to overcome the menace of delay is a million dollar question? Nevertheless, some of the observations may be helpful to plug loopholes and looking for the resolve of this menace. For instance, to segregate/separate the structure of Trial Courts as exhaustive that the nature of cases for disposal can be easily segregated/separated and the specialized Trial Judges with expertise specialization in the nature of cases can be engaged for the quick disposal of cases; to discard the specious submissions/claims of political or some vested interests agencies both at the Center and the States that the structure of the Trial Courts cannot be separated as it would be against the existing legal system and it shall create financial problems; to strengthen the recent emerging changing perceptions of Law in India that lawmen are attempting to determine the extent to which modern law notions have penetrated the village and the degree of congruence between the value premises of the new legality and those of customary practice and as such to have an appropriate approach to a better understanding of the confrontation between traditional law ways and the modern law to investigate village client; to develop a systematic as well as scientific description of litigants in District and Munsiff Courts that would yield important information on the role of law in Indian (courts) modernization in lessening delays.

TABLE 4.13

Sl. No.	*Litigants before Town Court*	*Response Frequency*	*Response Percentage*
1.	Zamidars	—	—
2.	Land Holders	—	—
3.	Tillers	—	—
4.	Poor persons	—	—
5.	Peasents	—	—
6.	Money Lenders	—	--
7.	All the above	306	85.00
8.	No comments	54	15.00
	Total	360	100

Table 4.13 helps to understand status/nature of litigants who come to the town courts from the villages. Majority 306:85% Trial Courts Judges respondents are of the opinion that Zamindars, Landholders, Tillers of the soil, Poor persons seeking matrimonial maintenance, Peasants against village money-lenders, Money-lenders against peasants, while 54:15% only have not responded to this significant enquiry. Be that as it may, the only hope of the villagers by involving themselves with the modern town courts is to achieve "Justice" that would be not only quick but followed by simple procedures devoid of adversarial technicalities as well as corruptive processes.

Is the adversary process previewed as a modality for realizing justice? The majority responses 276:76.67% of the Trial Courts judges-respondents are in affirmative, while 54:15% have responded in the negative, and 30:08.33% have not been fair as well as fearless to respond either way. It may discern that the adversarial process is impediment in the swift, fair, fearless, reasonable and just disposal of cases.

What images of the modern lawgivers are carried back

TABLE 4.14

Sl. No.	Adversary process as a modality for realizing justice	Response Frequency	Response Percentage
1.	Yes	276	76.67
2.	No	54	15.00
3.	No Comment	30	08.33
	Total	360	100

TABLE 4.15

Sl. No.	Image of judiciary carried to the village	Response Frequency	Response Percentage
1.	Independence of trial court	—	—
2.	Integrity of Trial Judge	—	—
3.	Impartiality of Trial Judge	—	—
4.	Clean image of Trial Judge	—	—
5.	Corrupt image of Trial Judge	—	—
6.	All the above	282	78.33
7.	No comment	78	21.67
	Total	360	100

to the village? The answer to this significant question depends upon the attitudinal approach of the villagers that they gather during conviviality. Majority 282:78.33% Trial Courts Judges-respondents opine that the villagers carry mixed image of Trial Judiciary to the village, viz., independence of the Trial Courts, integrity of Trial Courts, impartiality of Trial Courts, clean image of Trial Courts, corrupt image of Trial Courts.

Is judicial administration faulty and face value favouritism of some judges of Subordinate Judiciary and/or Lawyers is another cause of denial of justice? Majority Trial Judges-respondents 198:55% significantly have been fair as well fearless enough to admit it in the affirmative. And, the responsibility for this could be either due to court staff or due to non-effectiveness of Trial Judges. Be that as it may,

TABLE 4.16

Sl. No.	Favouritism as cause of denial of justice	Response Frequency	Response Percentage
1.	Yes	198	55.00
2.	No	102	28.33
3.	No Comment	60	16.67
	Total	360	100

TABLE 4.17

Sl. No.	Responsibility of Court Staff for favouritism	Response Frequency	Response Percentage
1.	Yes	24	12.12
2.	No	54	27.28
3.	No Comment	120	60.60
	Total	198	100

the cause of denial of justice due to "faulty judicial administration" and "face value favourtism" of some Judges of Subordinate Courts and Lawyers practicing therein can be approached either from the perspective of the professionals who transmit the modern legal culture—the judicial administration and legal practitioners—or of those who may receive it—to the clients. Further, the reasons for this are not far to seek because they are inherent/hidden in some penetrating questions, viz., how shall we investigate the impact of the modern legal culture on the Indian populace?, or, How widely disseminated are the Trial Courts decisions and how well observed and enforced are the rules embodied in them?, or, Can the Courts and lawyers help to inculcate beliefs and habits of political behaviour appropriate to constitutionalism?, or, What is being taught about the "Rule of Law" and the "role of law" by whom and to whom?

5

Court Management

Court Management is a juristic technique as well as art. Court management does not mean to bureaucratize the system and make it to be known as "juristocratic" institution. Court Management and Case Management are correlated to maximize efficiency and minimize deficiency. Court management and case management have varied dimensions. Court management and case management seem to be the sole soul of judicial process devoid of juristocratic recidivist deviance in decision-making process. There is dearth of literature in this perspective as no direct study material is available on the theme of court management. The common law models, already discussed, of U.K. (Lord Woolf's Report) and U.S.A. (Judge Ms. Ferm M. Smith) cannot be considered as well as conceded to be conducive to Trial Judiciary in Indian situations.[1] Some passing references on the theme are available in the Reports of the Law Commission of India.[2]

1. *Lord Justice Woolf's Report,* Access to Justice, *1966; Judge Ms. Ferm M. Smith, Educating The Judiciary, Span, Jan.-Feb. 2001.*
2. 117th Report 1986: Training of Judicial Officers; 131st Report 1988: Role of the Legal Profession in the Administration of Justice; 129th Report 1988: Urban Litigation Mediation as Alternative to Adjudication; 120th Report 1987: Manpower Planning in Judiciary: A Blueprint; 127th Report 1988: Resource Allocation for Infrastructure Services in Judicial Administration.

Be that as it may, the First National Judicial Pay Commission, famously known as Justice Jagannatha Shetty Report, has endeavoured for the first time to have in depth insights into the inquisitiveness of court management in quest of judicial reforms at Subordinate Courts level which is the citadel of the Indian Judiciary.[3] In the backdrop of it, Shetty Commission conceded "Improving Work Methods and Work Environment in the Subordinate Courts in India"[4] as a milestone in the court management, and to streamline court management it advocated for holding the "National Consultative Activity on Judicial Education and Training and I.T. for Judiciary".[5]

The general concept of court management is that the cases at the trial level are managed in such a way that cases at trial level are disposed off efficiently, effectively, speedily with the sensitivity of fair trial and fair justice with least bottlenecks. But, the trial courts function under strains, handicaps, hapless conditions, and as such there appears to be delay in the disposal of cases. There seems to be the handicaps in the form of functional independence as well as infrastructure facilities. However, both are dependent on the executive decision as well as whims of the executive.[6]

It has unequivocally been opined that court management and case management require the induction of new technologies of training to the trial judges either at the induction level or periodical refresher courses to update their knowledge with techniques of fast track disposal.[7] However, the experiences are that the trial Judges apply the same old procedure and same old court management and case management mechanisms.[8] It is a paradox that there seems no Information Technology for court management and case management; there is no Data Base application for cases; no

---

3. Government of India, The First National Judicial Pay Commission Report, Justice Jagannatha Shetty,2002.
4. *Ibid.*
5. *Ibid.*
6. *Ibid.*
7. *Ibid.*
8. *Ibid.*

Scanner or Electronic Filing for retrieving Documents, the means and methods used in almost all the industrial houses and business establishments.[9] Our trial Judiciary works in an antiquated atmosphere/system, and, therefore, there is a fast track needs to overhaul it lest it becomes bankrupt.

The technological developments, viz., information technology and computers, have made a turning point in the history of human civilization as well as every walk of human activity culminating in enhanced efficiency, productivity and quality. Similarly, inclusion of Information Technology (I.T.) Action Plan is imperative in judicial administration of subordinate courts in India. The utility of computerization of trial courts is *sine qua non* for the court work and court management for the purposes of improvements in operational efficiency, coordination, accessibility, and speed in the judicial administration and court as well as case management.[10] I.T. will minimize bottlenecks, delays, arrears and backlogs. I.T. will help to develop sound judicial management information system, case management and file-management, Docket-management in the Trial Courts. However, computer and confusion should neither be predicament nor be contentious in India in the Trial Courts in India.

TABLE 5.1

Sl. No.	Time of departure of office staff	Response Frequency	Response Percentage
1.	1.30 p.m.	—	—
2.	2.00 p.m.	18	5.00
3.	3.00 p.m.	12	3.33
4.	4.00 p.m.	24	6.66
5.	5.00 p.m.	198	55.00
6.	6.00 p.m.	42	11.67
7.	No comment	66	18.34
	Total	360	100

9. *Ibid.*
10. *Ibid.*

The first thing in court management is to comply with components of Trial Courts, viz., office clerk, office steno, office peon, case caller, etc. and in their efficiency lies the efficiency of court management in all its dimensions be that court discipline or court decorum or court record or case record or case docket or Trial Judge-Lawyer-client-public relationship. Besides, observance of office as well as court timings is imperative in court management. Both the Trial Judge and the office staff attached with the Trial Courts have to maintain office timings discipline, because it's violation ultimately affect the case rate disposal. Time of departure of office staff from the Trial Court is inasmuch as important as the in time arrival of office staff in the Trial Court is *sine qua non.* Court timings vary from place to place. In some places it is 8 a.m. to 1.30 p.m. in summer, and 10 a.m. to 4 p.m. in winter. In some places it is 10 a.m. to 5 p.m. all over the season. It has been observed that some of the office staff maintain office timings strictly and do not like either reaching late in office or leaving early from the office, but for some reaching late and leaving early is a rule than exception. It has been observed that some of the office staff leaves the court late if the Trial judge happens to leave late because such judge sits late in the court office to preparing his own briefs in the form of either his notes of the next days case docketed or his brief notes in preparing the judgments of already finally heard cases. The data presented in this Table as such shows the variance in time of departure.

TABLE 5.2

Sl. No.	*Time of arrival of Judge in Court*	*Response Frequency*	*Response Percentage*
1.	8 a.m.	36	10
2.	9 a.m.	30	08.33
3.	10 a.m.	216	60.00
4.	11 a.m.	—	—
5.	No comment	78	21.67
	Total	360	100

As already stated above, office timings of courts vary from place to place. It has been observed that the Trial Judges strictly adhere to court timings. But exceptions are also there of habitual late arrivals amongst Trial Judges as there is habit amongst the office staff, and this may be the impetus downward from the upward. Be that as it may, the Trial Courts that observe office timings from 10 a.m. to 5 p.m., the Trial Judges in majority 216:60% are habitual by habit as well as *Dharma* to strictly adhere to office timings.

TABLE 5.3

Sl. No.	*Time of departure of Judge from court*	*Response Frequency*	*Response Percentage*
1.	1.30 p.m.	—	—
2.	2.00 p.m.	—	—
3.	3.00 p.m.	18	5.00
4.	4.00 p.m.	36	10.00
5.	5.00 p.m.	198	55.00
6.	6.00 p.m.	48	13.33
7.	No comment	60	16.67
	Total	360	100

As already explained above, it is interesting to note that Trial Judges rarely leave court office as soon as it is off. But they remain in the Trial Courts for hours together even after the court timings not as time thriftier but doing some productive court work as already state above.

TABLE 5.4

Sl. No.	*Trial Court's timing*	*Response Frequency*	*Response Percentage*
1.	8 a.m. to 2 p.m.	312	86.67
2.	9 a.m. to 4 p.m.	—	—
3.	10 a.m. to 5 p.m.	48	13.33
6.	10 a.m. to 5.30 p.m.	—	—
	Total	360	100

The data presented in Table 5.4 relates to office timings of Trial Courts, and as already stated above the court timings vary from place to place.

TABLE 5.5

Sl. No.	Time taken by Trial Judge in occupying Court office	Response Frequency	Response Percentage
1.	Less than 15 minutes	126	35.00
2.	15 to 20 min.	36	10.00
3.	20 to 25 minutes	12	03.33
4.	25 to 30 minutes	84	23.34
5.	More than 30 minutes	66	18.33
6.	No comment	36	10.00
	Total	360	100

In Trial Courts management every minute is imperative in relation to disposal of cases and a single minute lost eventually affect the case-rate disposal. Therefore, it was necessary to know how much time does the Trial Judge take to come to Court Room from his Court Office after arriving at Court Office? Response frequency of the Trial Judges-respondents is not only interesting but intriguing also. Though in majority 126:35% Trial Judges take less than 15 minutes time in occupying Court Rooms after arriving at Court Offices, but rest of the responses speak volume. More the time consumed in movement from Court Offices to Court Rooms ultimately telling upon the case-rate disposal, viz., causing delay in the disposal of cases. This may also speak about the casual approach on the part of the Trial Judges to dispose of the cases belatedly or expeditiously as well as efficiently. Late arrival in Court Rooms may also yield less case-rate disposal.

However, it is interesting to note from the data presented in Table 5.6 that no Trial Judge leaves the Court Room any time during the proceedings of the case except only for lunch during lunch timing.

From the data presented in Tables 5.7 and 5.8 it is interesting to note that in majority 300:83.33% trial Judges do

TABLE 5.6

Sl. No.	Time at which Trial Judge leave the Court Room	Response Frequency	Response Percentage
1.	Any time during the proceedings of the case	—	—
2.	Only Lunch Time	324	90.00
3.	No comment	36	10.00
	Total	360	100

TABLE 5.7

Sl. No.	Leaving of Court Room in post lunch session for a break	Response Frequency	Response Percentage
1.	Yes	36	10.00
2.	No	300	83.33
3.	No Comment	24	06.67
	Total	360	100

TABLE 5.8

Sl. No.	Time for the Break	Response Frequency	Response Percentage
1.	Less than 15 minutes	12	33.33
2.	More than 15 minutes	24	66.67
3.	More than half an hour	—	—
	Total	36	100

not leave the Court Rooms in post lunch session for tea break, except an insignificant percentage 36:10% that breaks for tea in post lunch session and such presiding officers of Trial Courts consume less than 15 minutes or more than 15 minutes in sipping their cups of tea at the cost of court rooms timings.

Responses as to when do the Trial Judges close the court proceedings in post lunch session have been significant

TABLE 5.9

Sl. No.	Time of closing of Court proceedings in Post lunch session	Response Frequency	Response Percentage
1.	No proceedings are conducted in post lunch session	—	—
2.	At 3 p.m.	24	06.67
3.	At 4 p.m.	66	18.33
4.	At 5.p.m.	204	56.67
5.	No comment	66	18.33
	Total	360	100

to seek to. There is not even a single instance where no proceedings are being conducted in post lunch session. In almost in all the Trial Courts in India the proceedings are continuously conducted in post lunch session. Of course, the post lunch session proceedings may be short lived, or may continue for some hours depending upon the day's roaster, or may be for full time post lunch session. The research scholar observed that a Principal District Judge of Pune District Courts sits up to 5 p.m. and sometimes beyond that if the urgency of the case demands so though his subordinate judges do not seem to conduct court proceedings for such a long time in post lunch session. Be that as it may, in majority 204:56.67% the Trial Judges do conduct court proceedings up to 5 p.m. in post lunch session. The respondents who have not responded to this variable may be in a fix to give vent to truth.

TABLE 5.10

Sl. No.	Time spend in office to study cases after court proceedings	Response Frequency	Response Percentage
1.	Yes	324	90.00
2.	No	12	03.33
3.	No Comment	24	06.67
	Total	360	100

The response frequency significantly displays that in majority 324:90% they do spend time in office to study cases after court proceedings are complete. Though minority percentage of respondents 12:03.33% do not spend time in court offices to study cases after court proceedings, but the inferences are not insignificant. 24:06.67% have not responded, but it may discern that such respondents are afraid to share the truth of their career experiences in this perspective.

TABLE 5.11

Sl. No.	Time spent for study of court cases	Response Frequency	Response Percentage
1.	1 hour	144	40.00
2.	1 to 2 hours	126	35.00
3.	2 to 3 hours	36	10.00
4.	More than 3 hours	—	—
5.	No comment	54	15.00
	Total	360	100

In response to the data presented in Table 5.10, it was expediently imperative to know how much time does a Trial Judge spend in his court office to study court cases in order to comprehend them? Majority 144:40% spend not more than an hour daily to study the cases, 126:35% spend between 1-2 hours daily to study cases, whereas 36:10% spend 2-3 hours daily to study court cases.

TABLE 5.12

Sl. No.	Spending time in court office for writing judgments	Response Frequency	Response Percentage
1.	Yes	336	93.34
2.	No	6	01.66
3.	No Comment	18	05.00
	Total	360	100

336:93.34 Trial Court Judges-respondents do spend time in court offices for writing judgments, whereas insignificant number 6:01.66% of respondents do not spend time in court offices for writing judgments and the inferences in such cases may be varying, viz., it has been observed that such respondents take the refuge in senior counsels in writing judgments for and on their behalf. In one instance, a Trial/ Subordinate Judge happened to tell a senior counsel to write the judgment for and on his behalf and when that judgment was produced the Trial/Subordinate Judge had happened to tell such senior counsel to write the judgment in that language that may appear to had been written by the judge himself otherwise in appeal the High Court would pass strictures on the Trial Judge because such fascinating language he could not write. The Trial Court Judges who have unhesitatingly responded that they do spend time in court offices for writing judgments, and such Trial Judges spend between 1-4 hours for this purpose alone.

TABLE 5.13

Sl. No.	*Training of court staff to handle electronic gazettes*	*Response Frequency*	*Response Percentage*
1.	Yes	114	31.67
2.	No	234	65.00
3.	No Comment	12	03.33
	Total	360	100

The Trial Courts that have been adequately/sufficiently equipped with infrastructure facilities of modern scientific gazettes in terms of computer, internet, e-mail, fax, word processor, electronic typewriter, to handle court proceedings efficiently need trained court staff to handle such electronic gazettes. An in depth probing was done during interviews while gathering information on structured questionnaire, and the Trial Judges-respondents in majority 234:65% opined in the negative, while 114:31.67% replied in the affirmative. It is because of such negative response that electronic gazettes are lying unused in the Trial Courts either for the dust to pile therein or allowing the cobweb to make its way to weave an enchanting fabric. It may also discern that public money is not properly utilized. Computers have many facets/ dimensions for their use, but it has been observed that computers are being used as sophisticated typewriters.

TABLE 5.14

Sl. No.	Promotional avenues in career	Response Frequency	Response Percentage
1.	Yes	156	43.34
2.	No	174	48.33
3.	No Comment	30	8.33
	Total	360	100

The court staff that has been trained in the use of electronic gazettes does have (156:43.34%) promotional avenues in career. Those who opine otherwise (174:48.33%) do not see any promotional avenues in career advancement.

TABLE 5.15

Sl. No.	Lack of Govt. Interests in Court staff	Response Frequency	Response Percentage
1.	Yes	198	55.00
2.	No	60	16.66
3.	No Comment	102	28.34
	Total	360	100

Those respondents who have responded in the negative further opine that it only means that the irresponsible attitude of the government create disinterest in the office staff to discharge office duties efficiently to assist the Trial Judges to lessen/reduce the case load/piling of cases.

What is the attitude of the office staff towards the presiding officers of the Trial Court? The responses are both respectful and helping; a few members of the office staff

TABLE 5.16

Sl. No.	Attitude of Court staff towards presiding officer	Response Frequency
1.	Respectful and helping	306
2.	Respectful but not helping	—
3.	Helping	—
4.	Indifferent	—
5.	Working relationship	162
6.	Compromising	—
7.	Un-compromising	—
8.	Unhelpful	—
9.	Any other	—
	Total	468

maintain only working relationship. The court staff consists of all shapes and shades of religion, caste, and urban and rural, graduates/non-graduates.

TABLE 5.17

Sl. No.	Availability of services of scientific gazettes to complainants/clients	Response Frequency	Response Percentage
1.	Yes	138	38.33
2.	No	198	55.00
3.	No Comment	24	06.67
	Total	360	100

55% Trial Judges-respondents have expressed that the services of scientific gazettes are not made available to the complainants/clients, while 38.33% have responded that complainants/clients could make use of such scientific gazettes according to need and deed.

The data presented in Tables 5.18 and 5.19 pertain to bath rooms/toilets facilities for natural call made available to the Trial Judges, Advocates and particularly to the female

TABLE 5.18

Sl. No.	Facility of attached bathroom / Toilet to Trial Judge	Response Frequency	Response Percentage
1.	Yes	294	81.67
2.	No	24	06.67
3.	No Comment	42	11.66
	Total	360	100

TABLE 5.19

Sl. No.	Facility of attached bathroom/ Toilet to Advocates	Response Frequency	Response Percentage
1.	Yes	114	31.67
2.	No	234	65.00
3.	No Comment	12	03.33
	Total	360	100

advocates and visitors—male female both—coming to the Trial Courts for court works. The responses as presented above are encouraging, and where the responses are in the negative or with no comments are serious as well as meaningful, because bath rooms/toilets for natural calls particularly for female Advocates as well as female visitors to the Trial Courts are non-existent.

TABLE 5.20

Sl. No.	Library equipped with law literary	Response Frequency	Response Percentage
1.	Yes	234	65.00
2.	No	102	28.33
3.	No Comment	24	06.67
	Total	360	100

Trial Courts must be adequately equipped with law literary. Law literary must not become impediment in Trial Court process. The Trial Judges-respondents when asked pointedly on this parameter they were not only frank but fair as well as fearless in responding in majority voice 234:65% that Trial Courts have adequate law literary in terms of law reporters, and in almost all the Trial Courts contribute to A.I.R. as a chief source of law reference and precedent reference.

TABLE 5.21

Sl. No.	Time interval between cases filed and cases taken up for trial	Response Frequency	Response Percentage
1.	Less than a week	150	41.66
2.	1—2 weeks	12	03.34
3.	2—3 weeks	18	05.00
4.	3—4 weeks	6	01.66
5.	4—5 weeks	36	10.00
6.	More than 5 weeks	108	30.00
7.	No response	30	08.34
	Total	360	100

Time interval between cases filed and cases taken up for trial is an important barometer to measure delay in the disposal of cases at the root level. The Trial Judges in majority 150:41.66% have fairly expressed that they take less than a week's time for trial process, 108:30% take more than 5 weeks' time for trial process, and the rest take 1-2 weeks' time (12:03.34%), 2-3 weeks' time (18:05%), 3-4 weeks' time (6:01.66%), and 4-5 weeks' time (36:10%) for trial process.

Unreasonable gap of time interval between the acceptance of the case in the court office and taken up for trial process appears to be the basis/foundation for delay in the disposal of cases. And, the Trial Judges-respondents in majority 228:63.34% have been fair enough to admit it. Of course, 126:35% do not subscribe to it.

Time gestate is another important variable in measuring delay in the disposal of cases at the Trial Courts level, and as

TABLE 5.22

Sl. No.	Time consumption in acceptance and taken up for trial is cause of delay	Response Frequency	Response Percentage
1.	Yes	228	63.34
2.	No	126	35.00
3.	No Comment	06	01.66
	Total	360	100

TABLE 5.23

Sl. No.	Time consumed by court office in preparing the papers to be placed before Trial Judge	Response Frequency	Response Percentage
1.	Less than a week	216	60.00
2.	1—2 weeks	18	05.00
3.	2—3 weeks	—	—
4.	3—4 weeks	06	01.66
5.	4 weeks and more	120	33.34
	Total	360	100

such a probing deemed essential to know from the Trial Judges about the variable: 'Once the trial process is over, the papers have to be prepared by the court office, how much time the court office consumes in preparing the papers to be placed before the Trial Judge for finally writing the judgment? Majority respondents 216:60% have responded that court office staff takes less than a week's time in preparing the papers to be placed before the Trial Judges for writing judgment after the cases are finally heard. However, 120:33.34% respondents have acknowledged that court office staff takes 4 and more than 4 weeks' time in preparing the papers to be presented before the Trial Judges for writing judgments after the cases have been finally heard. This time gestate may be conceded the cause of influence by the contesting/litigious parties, or corruption of court office staff by the contesting/litigious parties to seeking favours indirectly from the presiding officers of the Trial Courts. Both these factors do affect the reputation, independence of the trial judiciary. Corruption is rampant in the society, and is of cancerous growth, and trial judiciary is not escape from this contagious decease. Corruption free trial judiciary could only be conceded as the least dangerous branch of the governmental organ, because it is the trustee of people's faith, and once the faith is belied its stature is belittled. Therefore, there has to be judicial accountability and transparency norms. In order to check incidents of growing corruption or indolent in the trial judiciary, it is up to the judiciary to do some soul searching to restitute judicial credibility. Corruption free trial judiciary can alone do justice, and there is nothing pretentious about it, in the real sense.

TABLE 5.24

Sl. No.	*Complicacy in Trial procedure*	*Response Frequency*	*Response Percentage*
1.	Yes	264	73.34
2.	No	48	13.33
3.	No Comment	48	13.33
	Total	360	100

Besides the time gestation, complexities of procedural laws are equally responsible for belated trial process. Adversarial process makes the trial procedure complicated. New cases are born out of the original suit/case and it first consumes time to settle such suits/cases than settling the original suit/case. The Trial Judges-respondents have also replied in the affirmative 264:73.34% and corroborated the variable that trial procedures are complicated. Various causes could be attributed to it, viz., procedural laws are adversarial in nature inasmuch as that the litigious parties to the suits/cases have had to prove to win the suits/cases and the courts have not be inquisitorial in their approach. The only conducive solution seems to be to simplify the trial procedures so that trial process consumes less time for the disposal of cases/complaints.

TABLE 5.25

Sl. No.	Frequency of transfer of court office staff	Response Frequency	Response Percentage
1.	One year	06	01.67
2.	Two years	84	23.33
3.	Three years	102	28.33
4.	Four years	24	06.66
5.	Five years	66	18.33
6.	More than five years	12	03.34
7.	No response	66	18.33
	Total	360	100

Frequency of Trial Courts office staff is an integral part of Trial Court management and human resource development. The process of transfer of court staff may sometimes hamper the office working or may sometimes contribute efficient office working. Be that as it may, the Trial Courts Judges-respondents have responded that in majority 102:28.33% court office is transferred once in three years, while 84:23.33% have opined that court office staff is transferred once in two years, 66:18.33% say that court office staff is transferred at an interval of five years period.

TABLE 5.26

Sl. No.	Frequency of transfer of Trial Court Judge	Response Frequency	Response Percentage
1.	One year	—	—
2.	Two years	—	—
3.	Three years	204	56.67
4.	Four years	18	05.00
5.	Five years	78	21.67
6.	More than five years	—	—
7.	No response	60	16.66
	Total	360	100

In order to improve efficiency and streamline the Trial Courts, transfer of Trial Court Judges is an integral part of court management. The transfer of Trial Judges is imperative so that politicking/monopolization is minimized/ruled out/ameliorated. The respondents in majority 204:56.67% have responded that Trial Judges are transferred once in three years period, 78:21.67% have expressed that transfer of Trial Judges from one Trial Court to another Trial Court inter-state takes place once in five years period.

TABLE 5.27

Sl. No.	Distribution of work load and management	Response Frequency	Response Percentage
1.	Strongly agree	204	56.67
2.	Agree	156	43.33
3.	Strongly disagree	—	—
4.	Disagree	—	—
5.	No response	—	—
	Total	360	100

204:56.67% Trial Judges-respondents strongly agree and 156:43.33% only agree that the distribution of the work load or systematization of the work load is the background of court management and is determined by the number of working units available with the Trial Court Judges. None of the respondents have expressed disagreement with it.

TABLE 5.28

Sl. No.	Desirability of reforms in Court administration	Response Frequency	Response Percentage
1.	Strongly agree	186	51.67
2.	Agree	96	26.66
3.	Strongly disagree	—	—
4.	Disagree	—	—
5.	No response	78	28.67
	Total	360	100

Likewise, 186:51.67% and 96:26.66% Trial Judges-respondents either strongly agree or only agree that there seems urgent desirability of reforms in Trial Court administration, and such response pattern confirms that in order to make the trial judicial process swift and just, a fresh approach to judicial administration by promoting court reforms through improvements in general administration is inevitable. Those who have not responded (78:28.67%) may not have appreciated the contents of innovative approach to bringing in reforms in trial courts administration for making trial judicial process swift and just? Why improvements in general administration of trial courts not coming up to the expectations? The reasons for this are not far to seek. The most conceptualized reason seems to be that in keeping with traditional concepts of an independent judiciary the Trial Courts have been left largely to their own devices to solve administrative problems and to initiate the reforms. But the Trial Courts have not taken enough initiations to solve their own problems, and as such the Parliamentarians as well as the State legislatures have been indifferent to the few proposals for reforms that have been brought forth.

TABLE 5.29

Sl. No.	*Pendency of cases is the cause for delay*	*Response Frequency*	*Response Percentage*
1.	Strongly agree	198	55.00
2.	Agree	60	16.66
3.	Strongly disagree	—	—
4.	Disagree	30	08.34
5.	No response	72	20.00
	Total	360	100

Piling of cases manifestly and undoubtedly seems to be the main cause of delay in the disposal of cases at the trial level on the one hand, and may be the death knell of the trial judicial process on the other hand. 198:55% and 60:16.66% Trial Judges-respondents either strongly agree or only agree with the statement that statistics of backlog and fresh cases indicate that existing administrative procedures as well as practices of all Trial Courts are not adequate to cope with ever growing case loads and as such many litigants are faced with intolerable delay. However, those Trial Judges-respondents who disagree (30:08.34%) with it intriguingly seem to be not accepting the reality of the complaint against the system and trying to make us believe the truth of their lies by expressing their disagreement with the most accepted/acknowledged complaint not refuted so far. Similar inferences may be advanced against those who have not responded to it (72:20%).

TABLE 5.30

Sl. No.	*Increase in number of judges is no solution*	*Response Frequency*	*Response Percentage*
1.	Strongly agree	24	06.66
2.	Agree	—	—
3.	Strongly disagree	—	—
4.	Disagree	216	60.00
5.	No response	120	33.34
	Total	360	100

Present strength of Trial Judges is inadequate to meet the challenges of millions of cases pending in the Trial Courts for swift and just disposal in the country, and the disposal rate is not justly keeping with the pace swiftness. The slow trial process is responsible for non-transparency in the trial judicial process. With the case growth there ought to be trial judge growth and that alone can solve the problem of challenges haunting the trial courts. 216:60%, therefore, disagree with the statement that the experiences indicate that adding more Trial Judges/creating Fast Track Courts can at times be no solution to the challenges at all. Those who strongly agree 24:06.66% with the statement perhaps do not appreciate the tone, letter and spirit of the challenges presently faced by the Trial Courts in the country. Similarly, those who have not responded perhaps do not wish to accept the reality of increase in the number of trial judges of trial courts to justly cope up with the swift and just disposal of cases devoid of piling of cases as well as delay in the disposal of cases, or increase in number of trial courts/fast track courts qualitatively and quantitatively.

TABLE 5.31

Sl. No.	Capability of Trial Courts to settle cases	Response Frequency	Response Percentage
1.	Strongly agree	216	60.00
2.	Agree	54	15.00
3.	Strongly disagree	06	01.66
4.	Disagree	30	08.34
5.	No response	36	10.00
	Total	360	100

It should not be concluded pre-maturely that Trial Courts are incapable of serving as a forum for peaceful settlement of disputes in an increasingly complex world. 75% refute the charge that trial courts are incapable of serving as a forum for peaceful, just, fair, reasonable and swift settlement of disputes in an increasingly complex world where new nature of disputes are increasing, rather these respondents agree that the trial courts in India are capable enough to meet the challenges of complexities of complex laws with the introduction of new nature of cases in an increasingly complex world. Those who have disagreed (36:10%) with it perhaps do not understand the import of this complexity and having or reposing faith in the Indian Trial Courts Judicial Process to face challenges presented by the new complex world legal order.

76.67% Trial Judges-respondents have expressed that they are in complete agreement with the statement that in order to overcome the problem of congestion and delay three important steps in Trial Court Management and Trial Court Administration must be taken, viz., (a) each Trial Court system must have a Supervisory Judge with the power and personnel to make and implement administration devices;

TABLE 5.32

Sl. No.	Delay and court management	Response Frequency	Response Percentage
1.	Strongly agree	216	60.00
2.	Agree	60	16.67
3.	Strongly disagree	—	—
4.	Disagree	—	—
5.	No response	84	23.33
	Total	360	100

(b) each Trial Court system must establish procedure to collect and analyze detailed current information about all relevant aspects of the Trial Courts' operations; and (c) each Trial Court system must have adequate facilities, competent clerical personnel, and office procedures that promote the efficient administration of justice for sound Judicial Management/administration.

TABLE 5.33

Sl. No.	Reluctance to seek services of management consultants in judicial system	Response Frequency	Response Percentage
1.	Strongly agree	174	48.34
2.	Agree	36	10.00
3.	Strongly disagree	06	01.66
4.	Disagree	—	—
5.	No response	18	05.00
	Total	360	100

Trial Courts lack management/administration and human resource development because of reluctance on the part of Trial Court Judges to seek services of management consultants in judicial system on the whole. Modern techniques of office management/human resource development inasmuch apply to the trial courts as those apply to the office management. The Law and Justice Ministry has to evolve as well as ensure an inbuilt mechanism to introduce new skills in Trial Courts management thus enabling the trial judges not having any inhibitions to seek services of management consultants to improving trial courts office management. One must not be hesitant to seek knowledge from any source it may come to improving the trial judicial and office management. 58.34% of Trial Judges-respondents have no inhibitions to agree that Trial Judges reluctance to make use of the services of Management Consultants has been a stumbling block in the improvement of Trial Courts and office management that is in part due to the lawyers' traditional distrust of methods that are new and strange.

TABLE 5.34

Sl. No.	*Ambiguity in utility of management consultants*	*Response Frequency*	*Response Percentage*
1.	Strongly agree	174	48.34
2.	Agree	36	10.00
3.	Strongly disagree	12	03.33
4.	Disagree	—	—
5.	No response	138	38.33
	Total	360	100

Why Trial Judges have been reluctant to make use of the services of Management Consultants? It may appear that the Management Consultants themselves have not addressed this question properly. The Management Consultants themselves have not made their usefulness clear to the Judiciary. They have failed to explain in cogent terms just what their studies can accomplish. They have failed to assuage the fear of the Legal Fraternity that "efficiency experts" will be unable to distinguish between delays in the Trial Judicial process that serves the ends of Justice and delays that are unnecessary and avoidable by improved management. 210:58.34% have fairly opined that ambiguity in management consultants is the basic cause of non-consultancy of management consultants by the trial judiciary.

TABLE 5.35

Sl. No.	Co-operation between Trial Court Judges and management consultants	Response Frequency	Response Percentage
1.	Strongly agree	174	48.33
2.	Agree	60	16.67
3.	Strongly disagree	—	—
4.	Disagree	06	01.67
5.	No response	120	33.33
	Total	360	100

In order to remove the gaps between the Trial Courts and the Management Consultants there has to be improvements in co-operation and coordination between the two inasmuch as the Trial Courts and the consultants have to recognize each other's needs and potentialities, they can co-operate to make the Trial Judicial System a modern instrument of Justice. 65% of the respondents have not refuted it.

TABLE 5.36

Sl. No.	Trial Calendar and Trial Court Judge	Response Frequency	Response Percentage
1.	Strongly agree	192	53.33
2.	Agree	114	31.66
3.	Strongly disagree	—	—
4.	Disagree	06	01.67
5.	No response	48	13.33
	Total	360	100

In order to plug loopholes in trial court management and streamline the trial court management, it is imperative that the Trial Courts control over the trial calendar should be vested in the Trial Court Judges. 306:84.99% Trial Judges-respondents agree with it. Those who have not responded, perhaps, do not wish to plug loopholes and improve Trial Court management.

TABLE 5.37

Sl. No.	Harmony between Lawyers and Courts	Response Frequency	Response Percentage
1.	Strongly agree	252	70.00
2.	Agree	78	21.66
3.	Strongly disagree	—	—
4.	Disagree	—	—
5.	No response	30	08.33
	Total	360	100

Another step forward in improving Trial Court management is in the harmony between lawyers and trial courts, viz., the lawyers should support the authority of the Court and the dignity of the Trial Court Room by strict adherence to the rules of decorum and by manifesting an attitude of professional respect toward the Trial Judge, opposing Counsel, witnesses, defendants, and others in the Court Room. 91.66% Trial Judges-respondents agree with it.

TABLE 5.38

Sl. No.	Improvement in the number of competent judges for prompt and fair administration of justice	Response Frequency	Response Percentage
1.	Strongly agree	240	66.66
2.	Agree	90	25.00
3.	Strongly disagree	12	03.34
4.	Disagree	—	—
5.	No response	18	05.00
	Total	360	100

Improvement in the number of competent Trial Court Judges is *sine qua non* for prompt and fair administration of justice, for the heart of the judicial process is the trial. The trial is based essentially in an adversary system of procedure. Although the Trial Courts in dense centers of population are plagued with ever mounting case loads, deteriorating physical facilities, insufficient, inefficient time spendthrifts personnel no Trial Courts anywhere in the country compare in importance with them from the standpoint of inculcating confidence in the judicial system for vast number of our citizens. There is, therefore, a necessity to provide judicial manpower. A sufficient, competent as well as efficient number of Trial Judges should be provided for each Judicial District to assure for the prompt and fair administration of justice. The data presented in this Table shows not fallacious but just response of the Trial Judges-respondents who in majority 330:91.66% have expressed their strong agreement with the above mentioned observations on the dismal picturesque functioning of the trial judiciary in the country.

TABLE 5.39

Sl. No.	*Facilities in Trail Court*	*Response Frequency*	*Response Percentage*
1.	Strongly agree	276	76.67
2.	Agree	78	21.67
3.	Strongly disagree	—	—
4.	Disagree	—	—
5.	No response	06	01.66
	Total	360	100

There is impending need of adequacy of courtroom facilities and supporting staff in order to improve trial court management vis-à-vis human resource management. The Trial Judges should be provided with courtroom facilities that are dignified and functional to assure the prompt and fair administration of justice. 354:98.34% Trial Judges-respondents have neither refuted nor expressed any reservations to it rather they have strongly agreed with it.

TABLE 5.40

Sl. No.	Co-operation between Judiciary, Executive and Legislature for proper administration of justice	Response Frequency	Response Percentage
1.	Strongly agree	216	60.00
2.	Agree	90	25.00
3.	Strongly disagree	30	08.33
4.	Disagree	12	03.34
5.	No response	12	03.34
	Total	360	100

In order to obtain the above mentioned or above set forth objectives, the Trial Judge has an obligation to seek the co-operation of the executive and legislative departments to provide judicial manpower, supporting staff, physical facilities, and adequate budget, because co-operation and coordination between judiciary, executive and legislature are effective instruments for proper administration of justice in democracy-judiciary lock jack. 306:85% Trial Judges-respondents have agreed/strongly agreed with it.

TABLE 5.41

Sl. No.	Trial Court judge's conversancy with inherent powers	Response Frequency	Response Percentage
1.	Strongly agree	252	70.00
2.	Agree	84	23.34
3.	Strongly disagree	06	01.66
4.	Disagree	—	—
5.	No response	18	05.00
	Total	360	100

In order to attain the above-mentioned objectives, the Trial Judges should be familiar with the nature and extent of the inherent power of the Judiciary to compel agencies of government to provide for staff, physical facilities, infrastructure, and funds. 336:93.34% Trial Judges-respondents strongly agree with it.

TABLE 5.42

Sl. No.	Trial Judge and control of the Court staff	Response Frequency	Response Percentage
1.	Strongly agree	252	70.00
2.	Agree	84	23.34
3.	Strongly disagree	06	01.66
4.	Disagree	—	—
5.	No response	18	05.00
	Total	360	100

Efficiency in trial court management lies with the managerial acumen of the Trial Judge to deal with the court staff. The Trial Judge has the duty to have the court staff properly trained and under his effective control. 336:93.34% Trial Judges-respondents strongly agree with it.

TABLE 5.43

Sl. No.	Trial Judge and the reporter	Response Frequency	Response Percentage
1.	Strongly agree	234	65.00
2.	Agree	108	30.00
3.	Strongly disagree	—	—
4.	Disagree	06	01.66
5.	No response	12	03.34
	Total	360	100

Another significant aspect of Trial Court management is that the Trial Judge has a duty to see that the reporter makes a true, complete and accurate record of all proceedings with professional independence. Retrieval and preservation of court records accurately is *sine qua non* of judicial process. 342:95% trial Judges-respondents strongly agree with it.

The Trial Court Judge has the ultimate responsibility for the docket, i.e., for proper management of calendar in criminal cases and civil suits. 354:98.34% Trial Judges-respondents strongly agree with it.

TABLE 5.44

Sl. No.	Trial Court Judge and the docketing	Response Frequency	Response Percentage
1.	Strongly agree	246	68.34
2.	Agree	108	30.00
3.	Strongly disagree	—	—
4.	Disagree	06	01.66
5.	No response	—	—
	Total	360	100

TABLE 5.45

Sl. No.	Trial Court Judge's power to regulate discussion amongst counsels	Response Frequency	Response Percentage
1.	Strongly agree	234	65.00
2.	Agree	120	33.33
3.	Strongly disagree	—	—
4.	Disagree	—	—
5.	No response	06	01.66
	Total	360	100

To ensure Trial Court management discipline, the Trial Court Judge should make known before trial that no colloquy, argument or discussion takes place directly between counsels in the presence of the Trial Court Judge, and 354:98.34% Trial Judges-respondents have opined strong agreement with it with negligible refutation of response.

6

Delay: Attitudes, Habits, Tenure and Filing of Cases

Delay is a riddle wrapped in mystery inside an enigma[1]. There may be multifarious dimensions for the occurrence of delay in the disposal of cases at the trial court level, but there are no fixed units of measurements for delay. The general concept is that the cases at the trial level are managed in such a way that cases at trial level are disposed off efficiently, effectively, speedily with the sensitivity of fair trial and fair justice with least bottlenecks. But, the trial courts function under strains, handicaps, hapless conditions, case load crisis, and as such there appears to be delay in the disposal of cases. There is the impression that juristocratic recidivism deviance attitude of lawmen may be the causal factor for delay and that the trial judiciary has been misunderstood. There is also a complaint that instead of trial judges managing the cases, the lawyers have purloined the 'court and case management' and, hence, delay. For the trial judge, court and case management problems are grave and great and are due to the mutation in the character of cases since the civil and criminal litigation have evolved into complex proceedings, full of adversaries, interstices, pretrial

1. K.L. Bhatia, *et. al.* J.I.L.I., 1995.

problems, discoveries, allegiance to indecisiveness and disinterestedness and culminating in lengthening trial as well as delay in disposal of cases.[2] Therefore, the role and responsibilities of trial judges are not to be underestimated or neglected, because trial courts are "trier of facts" and are the "first tier in the judicial system" or "upper court bias", and trial/lower courts Judges, in fact, handle the bulk of judicial business—including the management of case processing, approval of plea bargains, supervision of the settlement process, and monitoring remedial decrees—and experience the drama of the (trauma) of the adversary process.[3]

The trial court Judges though called as "adversary Judges" continue to work furiously, but they are unable to cope with the torrent of cases. The trial court Judges have to be virtuous, because that defines the qualities in terms of the personality of the trial/lower court Judge which may be ineluctable, viz., neutral, detached, kindly, benign, reasonably learned in the law, firm but fair, assertive, flexible in rigidity, wise, knowledgeable about human behaviour, independence, courtesy and patience, dignity, humourous, open-mindedness, impartiality, thoroughness, decisiveness, an understanding heart, social consciousness, and conscientious.[4] Be that as it may, are these virtuous qualities sustainable is a million dollar question, because had these been sustainable the trial court Judges could have been conceded angels. But men do not act like angels, and as such the trial Judge has a more robust part to play as a "non-contentious umpire standing between the adversary parties, seeing that they observe the rules of the adversary game. The bedrock premise is that the adversary contest is the ideal way to achieve truth and a just

---

2. See, Alvin B. Rubin, *Bureaucratization of the Federal Courts: The Tension Between Justice and Efficiency*, in Mark W. Cannon and David M.O. Brien (Ed.), Views from the Bench, 1987, p. 84.
3. *Id.*, p. 29.
4. *Id.*, p. 47; see also B. Sheintag, *The Personality of the Judge*, New York 1944; C. Wyzanski, *A Trial Judge's Freedom and Responsibility*, 65 *Harvard Law Review*, 1281 (1952); M. Rosenberg, *The Qualities of Justices—Are They Sustainable*, 44 Texas Law Rev., 1063 (1966); M. Frankel, *The Search For Truth: An Umperial View*, 123 University of *Pennsylvania Law Review*, 1031, 1041-45(1975).

result rested upon the truth."[5] However, if judging is to be done only by judges then essence of the judicial role of the trial judges is indeed "impartiality and detachment, both felt and exhibited",[6] in quest for truth and justice. And, concerned only that right is done by just ends and just means, the trial judge "should be patient, dignified, and courteous to litigants, witnesses, lawyers, and others as he presides over the contentious strivings towards that end".[7] Nevertheless, there is some tension as well as inconsistency between the professed ideals and the realities with the result that delay in the disposal of cases occur with the piling of cases in the trial/lower courts. It is being felt that piling of cases may yield death knell of the judicial system. It is no denying the fact that creating a workload now changes the very nature of trial courts, "threatening to convert them from deliberative institutions to processing institutions, from a judiciary to a bureaucracy . . . However efficient the judicial branch may become, it cannot mass-produce justice. Wise decisions cannot be made if cases come in vast numbers on judicial assembly line".[8]

In the backdrop of the above, it is evident that delay in disposal of cases is due to (a) pending of 23.9 million cases in India's 12,822 courts, including 12800 subordinate courts, 21 High Courts and the Supreme Court,[9] (b) endless adjournments and other sluggish ways of delaying justice, (c) corrupt judiciary and judicial officers,[10] and (d) shortage of judges.[11] Therefore, the felt need to revamp the trial judiciary is to weed out the deadwood and the corrupt and the

5. *Supra* note 3 at pp. 47-48.
6. *Ibid.*
7. *Ibid.*
8. *Ibid.*
9. See *The Daily Excellsior*, June 17, 2003. Around three crore cases are awaiting disposal in lower courts throughout the country. Fruits of changes in 93 old Code of Civil Procedure are yet to be felt. Complaints of 48 years, 47 years, 43 years and 42 years, etc. pending cases are yet to yield results.
10. *The Hindu* and *The Hindustan Times*, 24.9.2003.
11. *The Hindu*, 24.9.2003.

corruption from the corridors of the lower judiciary and to reinvest the trial judiciary with virtuous and quality judges.[12] It is also the felt necessity to remove snags in raising the strength of the trial/lower court Judges to dispense justice to the wronged, whose ranks continue to swell.[13] It is one of our biggest worries that paucity of judges in law courts in general and the subordinate/trial/lower courts in particular is the main cause for unconscionable delays in the disposal of cases and consequent build-up of arrears.[14] In proportion to its population, India is rated by experts to have among the lowest number of judges in the world, only 10.5 per million people in India as against 50.9 in Britain, 57.7 in Australia, 75.2 in Canada, and 107 in the United States. Be that as it may, it has been observed that the situation in trial/lower/ subordinate judiciary, the base of the entire judicial pyramid, is not any better.[15] It has suffered utter neglect be it be in matters of reforms, infrastructure, manpower, management, appointment of judges, filling of vacancies, provision of basic facilities to enable subordinate/lower/trial courts to function at reasonable levels of efficiency.[16] "It is a matter of shame that against a requirement of 75,000 judicial officers, the sanctioned strength of judges remain just 13,000. Out of this, 1,874 incumbents are working across the country. It means that 15 per cent of the courts where citizens seek justice at the first instance are headless".[17] The felt need for increasing the strength of trial Judges is to wipe out the mounting arrears and also to minimize or ameliorate delay.

Besides, the individual habits, too, play a subtle role in the building of a personality. Though, habits die hard, yet the habits of a trial judge as a person adorning the Bench develop his personality as a dispenser of justice. Habits, good or bad, develop a judicious thinking process, justice mind,

12. *The Hindustan Times*, 24.9.2003.
13. *The Hindu*, 24.9.2003.
14. *Ibid.*
15. *Ibid.*
16. *Ibid.*
17. *Ibid*

justice perceptions, justice vision, and cumulatively reflect decision-making process culminating into justice delivery system. Habits and personality go hand in hand to make a trial judge a great judge like the mighty jurists of yester years, he may not be a mere pen-pusher but the producer of great decisions, and as such a trial judge must have time to think, to ponder, to read and to write meaningfully.

TABLE 6.1

Sl. No.	*Length of service of Trial Court Judge*	*Response Frequency*	*Response Percentage*
1.	One year	—	—
2.	Two years	66	18.33
3.	Three years	36	10.00
4.	Four years	06	01.66
5.	Five years	06	01.66
6.	Six years	06	01.66
7.	Seven years	06	01.66
8.	Eight years	24	06.66
9.	Nine years	18	05.00
10.	More than Nine years	144	40.00
11.	No response	48	13.34
	Total	360	100

Attitudes, habits, tenure, filing of cases, may be attributed as units of measurement for determining delay taking place in the disposal of cases. Since how long as a Trial Judge has been occupying the position in the respective Trial Court? 144:40% have more than nine years length of service as Trial court Judge, 66:18.33% respondents have two years length of service as Trial Court Judge, 36:10% respondents have three years length of service as Trial Court Judge, 24:06.66% respondents have eight years length of service as Trial Court Judge, 18:05% respondents have nine years length of service as Trial Court Judge, and 24:06.66% of respondents length of service ranges between four to seven years respectively as Trial Court Judge. The variation in length of service shows the variation in experience, and the experience behaviour pattern may be the behavioural pattern for swift and just or delay/dilatory/time-wasting for the disposal of cases.

TABLE 6.2

Sl. No.	Time of getting up	Response Frequency	Response Percentage
1.	4 a.m.	—	—
2.	4.30 a.m.	—	—
3.	5.00 a.m.	60	16.67
4.	5.30 a.m.	102	28.34
5.	6.00 a.m.	144	40.00
6.	6.30 a.m.	24	06.66
7.	7.00 a.m. and afterwards	12	03.33
8.	No response	18	05.00
	Total	360	100

Freshness and fatigue depend on the behavioural pattern of getting up in the morning and retiring to bed for sleep in the night, and the working capacity also depend on it. To a question when do the Trial Judges-respondents get up in the morning, 144:40% have responded that they get up 6 a.m., 102:28.34% get up at 5.30 a.m., 60:16.67% have the habit to get up at 5 a.m. daily, 24:6.66% have the habit to get up at 6.30 a.m., and 12:03.33% have the habit to get up at 7 a.m. or even after 7 a.m.

TABLE 6.3

Sl. No.	Routine for morning walk	Response Frequency	Response Percentage
1.	Yes	204	56.67
2.	No	132	36.67
3.	No Comment	24	06.66
	Total	360	100

Morning walk, inhaling oxygen, yoga, pranayam, etc. help to keep a person fit, hale and hearty. 204:56.67% Trial

Judges—respondents have the habit to go for morning walk daily, while 132:36.67% have no habit to go for morning walk, and whereas 24:06.66% have no comments to make on their personal habit pattern for morning walk.

TABLE 6.4

Sl. No.	Routine for evening walk	Response Frequency	Response Percentage
1.	Yes	162	45.00
2.	No	174	48.33
3.	No Comment	24	06.67
	Total	360	100

Similarly, 162:45% Trial Judges-respondents have the habit to go for evening walk daily, while 174:48.33% respondents have not habit for evening walk. Those who do not go for evening walk prefer to spend their evenings in leisure time activities, and they have not liked to spell out their leisure time activities. Those who go for morning and evening walks have different habits of company for morning and evenings, viz., they may do so alone, or may like the company of their wives, or wives and children, or lacunae, i.e. lawyers/brethren/fellow trial judges, or with non-lacunae, or friends, i.e. law professionals/non-law professionals.

TABLE 6.5

Sl. No.	Routine for meditation in morning and evening	Response Frequency	Response Percentage
1.	Yes	306	85.00
2.	No	30	08.34
3.	No Comment	24	06.66
	Total	360	100

Meditation develops concentration; it may also be contributory for developing the notions of mediation as well as conciliation. Therefore, 306:85% Trial Judges-respondents have adapted a habit to do meditation both in the mornings and evenings to develop and increase concentration.

TABLE 6.6

Sl. No.	*Time to retire to bed*	*Response Frequency*	*Response Percentage*
1.	8 p.m.	—	—
2.	9 p.m.	—	—
3.	10 p.m.	54	15.00
4.	11 p.m.	234	65.00
5.	After 11 p.m.	54	15.00
6.	No response	18	05.00
	Total	360	100

Early to bed and early to rise makes man healthy, wealthy and wise. This proverbial habit is indeed a sound contributory factor in the development of the personality of a person, so is true with the trial judges, viz., ascendancy and descendants to attitudes, aptitudes, perceptions, visions, thinking process, assimilation and dissemination of knowledge, swinging or sinking or coming down from a certain intellectual moral or social standard, etc. depend upon this proverbial habit. In majority 234:65% Trial Judges-respondents have the habit to retire for bed at 11 p.m., 54:15% retire for bed at 10 p.m., and similar percentage of respondents retire for bed after 11 p.m.

TABLE 6.7

Sl. No.	*Daily routine of newspaper reading*	*Response Frequency*	*Response Percentage*
1.	Yes	318	88.33
2.	No	18	05.00
3.	No Comment	24	06.67
	Total	360	100

Do the trial judges read news paper(s) daily? Reading and assimilation habits inculcate to gaining knowledge and keeping oneself up to date with the new developments. 318:88.33% respondents read newspapers daily.

TABLE 6.8

Sl. No.	Reading of newspapers	Response Frequency
1.	Local	312
2.	National	312
3.	No Comment	48
	Total	672

312 respondents read both national as well as local news papers daily.

TABLE 6.9

Sl. No.	Preference of reading editorial views and articles	Response Frequency	Response Percentage
1.	Yes	252	70.00
2.	No	06	01.66
3.	No Comment	102	28.34
	Total	360	100

252:70% respondents prefer to read editorial views as well as articles while reading newspapers.

TABLE 6.10

Sl. No.	Enjoyment of reading editorial views and articles	Response Frequency	Response Percentage
1.	Yes	240	95.23
2.	No	12	04.77
3.	No Comment	—	—
	Total	252	100

240:95.23% of such respondents derive enjoyment while reading editorial views as well as articles.

TABLE 6.11

Sl. No.	*Watching television*	*Response Frequency*	*Response Percentage*
1.	Yes	330	91.67
2.	No	06	01.66
3.	No Comment	24	06.67
	Total	360	100

330:91.67% of the respondents watch television for varied purposes, viz., recreation, news listening, dramatic serials, discovery, etc.

TABLE 6.12

Sl. No.	*Preference of programmed viewing on T.V.*	*Response Frequency*	*Response Percentage*
1.	News	270	75.00
2.	Serials	—	—
3.	Movies	—	—
4.	Shastriya Sangeet	—	—
5.	Geetmala	30	08.34
6.	No response	60	16.66
	Total	360	100

270:75% Trial Judges-respondents prefer to view news programmes exhibited on televisions on different channels, 30:08.34% prefer to view 'geetmala' programmes, and 60:16.66% have no response to make.

Is in service Refresher Course in Law/Orientation Course in Law/Continuing Legal Education training through National Judicial Academy or State Judicial Academy imparted to the Trial Court Judges imperative to keep them abreast with modern developments of Law? 276:76.66% trial Judges-respondents have opined that this type of training is

TABLE 6.13

Sl. No.	Necessity for refresher course and orientation course for Trial Court judges	Response Frequency	Response Percentage
1.	Yes	276	76.66
2.	No	42	11.67
3.	No Comment	42	11.67
	Total	360	100

imperative as well as impending to increase qualitative Trial Judges in the wholesome of quantitative lot. Qualitative upwardness will certainly overhaul quantitative trial judiciary. Likewise, imparting of judicial training to clerical staff for judicial work is equally imperative to improve judicial system at trial court level, and this has been the opinion of the Trial Judges-respondents. In service judicial education and training and I.T. for Judiciary will certainly improve work methods and work environment in the Subordinate/Trial Courts in India.

TABLE 6.14

Sl. No.	Personal attendance in such a course	Response Frequency	Response Percentage
1.	Yes	108	39.13
2.	No	168	60.87
3.	No Comment	—	—
	Total	276	100

108:39.13% respondents have personally attended such legal training courses.

73:67.59% out of the abovementioned respondents have once attended such a legal training course during their total span of judicial career; 10:09.25 each have attended such legal training courses twice and thrice respectively during their total span of judicial career.

TABLE 6.15

Sl. No.	Number of times having attended the course	Response Frequency	Response Percentage
1.	One	73	67.59
2.	Two	10	09.25
3.	Three	10	09.25
4.	Four	—	—
5.	No response	15	13.91
	Total	108	100

TABLE 6.16

Sl. No.	Frequency of Training	Response Frequency	Response Percentage
1.	Once a year	30	17.78
2.	After every two years	—	—
3.	No Comment	78	72.22
	Total	108	100

What is the frequency of such a legal training? 30:17.78% have been judicious to say that such a legal training is held once a year, while intriguingly 78:72.22% of the respondents have no comments to offer in this perspective.

TABLE 6.17

Sl. No.	Language in which training course is conducted	Response Frequency	Response Percentage
1.	Hindi	18	05.00
2.	English	264	73.33
3.	Local language	12	03.34
4.	Both Hindi and English	—	—
5.	Both local and English	—	—
6.	No response	66	18.33
	Total	360	100

When asked in which language such continuing legal training is conducted, 264:73.33% Trial Judges-respondents have unequivocally have stated that legal training courses are conducted in English language, and 18:05% percentage have stated that such training is conducted in Hindi language, whereas 66:18.33% of the respondents have inhibitions to make any response to such an important query.

TABLE 6.18

Sl. No.	*Attachment of Law clerk with legal background with Trial Judge*	*Response Frequency*	*Response Percentage*
1.	Yes	228	63.33
2.	No	84	23.33
3.	No Comment	48	13.34
	Total	360	100

Attachment of Law Clerks with Trial or Higher Judiciary is an American concept. It has been tried at the Apex Court level during Justice P.N. Bhagwati, Justice R.S. Pathak, etc. tenures. Law Clerks help/assist Judges with new/innovative insights of legal knowledge they gain at Law Schools in the dispensation of justice. The Trial Judges were made to comprehend and appreciate the philosophy working behind the notion of Law Clerks. 228:63.33% percentage of the respondents have agreed that a provision for the attachment of a Law Clerk (who shall always be a fresh law graduate in first class from a Law College/Law School/Law Department of a University) with the Trial Court would essentially help the Trial Judges in swift, just and efficacious disposal of cases. However, 84:23.33% percentage of the respondents has not appreciated this perception. Perhaps, such of the respondents may not have appreciated/ comprehended the qualitative working spirit behind the notion.

The response frequency shows the nature of pendency of civil, criminal, matrimonial, and miscellaneous cases in the Trial Courts. 114:31.66% say that it is less than 1000 nature of suits/cases, 24:06.67% say it is more than 1000 nature of

TABLE 6.19

Sl. No.	Pendency of cases in Trial Court	Response Frequency	Response Percentage
1.	Less than 1000 civil cases Civil/ Criminal/Matrimonial cases	114	31.66
2.	More than 1000 civil cases Civil/ Criminal/Matrimonial cases	24	06.67
3.	No Comment	222	61.67
	Total	360	100

suits/cases, and 222:61.67% have no comments to make, because, either they do not know the quantity of pendency of suits/cases or they do not want to share the secrets of the quantity of pendency of suits/cases. Be that as it may, the magnitude pendency of suits/cases is the magnitude problem of piling of suits/cases in the Trial Courts in the country, and as such this magnitude problem of delay in the disposal of cases is plaguing the judicial system.

TABLE 6.20

Sl. No.	Disposal rate of cases	Response Frequency	Response Percentage
1.	Daily	48	13.33
2.	Weekly	12	03.33
3.	Monthly	—	—
4.	Yearly	—	—
5.	No response	300	83.34
	Total	360	100

Disposal rate of cases is significant in measuring the delay, and that depends upon the disposal rate of cases per day, per week, per month, and per year. The responses sought on this parameter have not been encouraging because majority respondents' 300:83.34% have not given any encouraging response in this perspective. Though the presiding officers of the trial courts dispose of the cases daily/weekly, but they have been silent to respond to disposal rate of cases that is *sine qua non* to measure delay.

TABLE 6.21

Sl. No.	Satisfaction with disposal rate of cases	Response Frequency	Response Percentage
1.	Satisfactory	120	33.33
2.	Above average	132	36.67
3.	Average	60	16.67
4.	Non satisfactory	—	—
5.	No response	48	13.33
	Total	360	100

Disposal rate of cases and satisfaction of presiding officers of the Trial Courts in regard to disposal rate is interlinked. 132:36.67% of the respondents feel that the disposal rate of cases is above average, 120:33.33% feel that the disposal rate of cases in the given circumstances, viz., Judge-Population-Case ratio, is somewhat satisfactory, 60:16.67% feel that disposal rate of cases is only average, and 48:13.33% do not feel to respond and that could be construed as their utter dissatisfaction or casual approach to the disposal rate of cases.

TABLE 6.22

Sl. No.	Rate of disposal and arrears of cases	Response Frequency	Response Percentage
1.	Increasing	270	75.00
2.	Decreasing	12	03.33
3.	No Comment	78	21.67
	Total	360	100

In the backdrop of the abovementioned disposal rate of cases, it seemed imperative to know in depth whether arrears/accumulation of cases with such a snail-race approach increasing or decreasing? Responses of the majority of the

Trial Judges-respondents have been on the right track that in the backdrop of snail-race approach arrears/accumulation of cases are speedily increasing, and those who have responded (12:03.33%) that arrears/accumulation of cases are decreasing their responses seem to be given in unmindful or casual approach. Keeping in view Justice Malimath Committee Report and Justice Shetty Report, it is impending to raise Judge : Case ratio and Judge : Population ratio in order to improve the case disposal rate as well as to minimize delay in the disposal of cases, and it may be worth if it is 50:100,000.

TABLE 6.23

Sl. No.	*Personal response as to accumulation of cases*	*Response Frequency*	*Response Percentage*
1.	Encouraged	18	05.00
2.	Discouraged	294	81.66
3.	No Comment	48	13.34
	Total	360	100

What seems to be the personal attitude of the Trial Judges relating to accumulation/piling of cases? Majority of the Trial Judges-respondents 294:81.66% have opined that they discourage accumulation/piling of cases in the Subordinate Courts because that affects to their name and fame and also to the name and fame of the Judicial system on the whole.

TABLE 6.24

Sl. No.	*Necessity of measures to overcome piling of cases*	*Response Frequency*	*Response Percentage*
1.	Yes	162	45.00
2.	No	—	—
3.	No Comment	198	55.00
	Total	360	100

What effective steps are necessary to overcome this problem of accumulating/piling of cases? What steps ought to be taken to keep the people aware about the accumulation of cases? 162:45% of the Trial Judges-respondents have the genuine feeling that there seems necessity of taking measures to overcome the problem of accumulation/piling of cases by educating the mind of the people through reporting in the media both local as well as national in order to plug loopholes and improving the work methods and work culture in the Subordinate/Trial Courts. Improvements in the work methods and work culture alone shall help to minimize the problem of accumulation/piling of cases in the Trial Courts which are otherwise alarming.

TABLE 6.25

Sl. No.	*Steps to make people aware about accumulation of cases*	*Response Frequency*	*Response Percentage*
1.	Education Through local Media	—	—
2.	Education Through National Media	—	—
3.	Both the above	240	66.66
4.	No comment	120	33.34
	Total	360	100

TABLE 6.26

Sl. No.	*Disposal rate is higher in pre—lunch in comparison to post—lunch session*	*Response Frequency*	*Response Percentage*
1.	Strongly agree	174	48.33
2.	Agree	54	15.00
3.	Strongly disagree	—	—
4.	Disagree	78	21.67
5.	No opinion	54	15.00
	Total	360	100

Another measurement to minimize/eradicate delay in disposal of cases is freshness of physique and mind. Hearing and disposal rate in pre-lunch session is swifter and just as compared to post lunch session. Pre-lunch session is fresh and post-lunch session is full of fatigue, and as such graph of disposal rate, it has been observed as well as experienced, in pre-lunch session is higher as compared to post-lunch session, that is fatigued session as per observation and experience, where graph of disposal rate is lower. 228:63.33% of the Trial Judges-respondents strongly agree and only agree that disposal rate is higher in pre-lunch session in comparison to post-lunch session. However, 78:21.67% of the Trial Judges-respondents disagree with it, and 54:15% of the respondents have no opinion to express in this perspective.

TABLE 6.27

Sl. No.	*Frequent holidays increase the pendency*	*Response Frequency*	*Response Percentage*
1.	Yes	312	86.66
2.	No	36	10.00
3.	No Comment	12	03.34
	Total	360	100

It has been the feeling that loss of man-days due to frequent holidays (National/State/Local) is the fountainhead cause for the occurrence of delay in the judicial process at the Trial Court level. 312:86.66% of the Trial Judges-respondents have affirmed that frequent holidays contribute to the piling of cases as well as delay in the disposal of cases.

258:71.67% of the respondents have agreed that it should be imperative to increase man-days in order to minimize piling of cases as well as delay.

How to overcome the menace of more holidays and less man-days? 282:78.33% of the Trial Judges-respondents have suggested that to cure this ailment it should be imperative to decrease the number of holidays that are allowed on petty matters, and only National holidays should be permitted and that shall be compatible with the new trends of work methods and work culture.

TABLE 6.28

Sl. No.	*To minimize piling of cases and delay increase of man—days should be imperative by curtailing holidays*	*Response Frequency*	*Response Percentage*
1.	Yes	258	71.67
2.	No	78	21.67
3.	No Comment	24	06.66
	Total	360	100

TABLE 6.29

Sl. No.	*Suggestions as to decrease in holidays*	*Response Frequency*	*Response Percentage*
1.	Decrease holidays on petty matters	186	51.67
2.	National holidays only to be provided	96	26.66
3.	No Comment	78	21.67
	Total	360	100

TABLE 6.30

S. No.	*Delay causes unpleasantness*	*Response Frequency*	*Response Percentage*
1.	Strongly agree	198	55.00
2.	Agree	120	33.34
3.	Strongly disagree	06	01.66
4.	Disagree	06	01.66
5.	No comment	30	08.34
	Total	360	100

Delay can be termed as a fountainhead of indecisiveness and indecisiveness causes unpleasantness. 318:88.34% Trial Judges-respondents are either in strong agreement with it or simply agree with it. Indecisiveness though may be a part of personality cult, but it, nevertheless, brings unpleasantness to all in the judicial process and eventually it affects the just disposal of cases at the trial courts.

TABLE 6.31

Sl. No.	Main cause of delay	Response Frequency
1.	Inadequate manpower	114
2.	Inefficient manpower	114
3.	In competitor manpower	114
4.	Frequent adjournments	318
	Total	660

What could be the fountainhead cause of delay at the trial courts level? In almost all the Trial Judges-respondents have penned down four chief causes of delay, viz., inadequate manpower, inefficient manpower, in competitor manpower, and frequent adjournments just on demand.

TABLE 6.32

Sl. No.	Delay is because of number of cases and number of appeals	Response Frequency	Response Percentage
1.	Yes	276	76.66
2.	No	72	20.00
3.	No response	12	03.34
	Total	360	100

276:76.66% of the respondents have expressed that delay in Trial Courts has become almost entirely identified with the problem of too many cases/suits flowing from the original parent case/suit and too many appeals. Most of the time—in years together—is consumed/wasted in disposal of secondary cases/suits emanating from the parent suits/cases and then reverting to the parent suits/cases for their disposal that again consumes unfathomable time. Consumption of unfathomable time in disposal of cases at the trial level itself is the death knell not only of the case but also of the judicial process.

TABLE 6.33

Sl. No.	*Delay can be eliminated by increasing the number of judges*	*Response Frequency*	*Response Percentage*
1.	Yes	288	80.00
2.	No	48	13.33
3.	No Comment	24	06.67
	Total	360	100

How to solve the riddle of delay? This question has been addressed time and again, and academia, jurists, justices and sociologists have been suggesting various measures to plug loopholes in the system. 288:80% of the respondents have agreed that the problem of delay can be eliminated if increasing the number of Trial judges keeping in mind the population explosion and case-population solves the problem of too many cases/suits emanating from the parent cases/ suits and too many appeals.

TABLE 6.34

Sl. No.	*Delay is because of lengthy procedure*	*Response Frequency*	*Response Percentage*
1.	Strongly agree	180	50.00
2.	Agree	162	45.00
3.	Strongly disagree	—	—
4.	Disagree	—	—
5.	No response	18	05.00
	Total	360	100

Delay in court process continues because the trial process of litigation is accusatorial and, because, is time consuming. The total workload of Trial Court is determined by the number of cases that have to be handled, multiplied by average amount of work that has to be performed in connection with each case. 342:95% Trial Judges-respondents agree with it inasmuch as that delay is because of lengthy procedure followed in the judicial process at the trials.

TABLE 6.35

Sl. No.	*Problems in terms of elimination of technicalities, formalisms, obstructive touts, etc. will alone help speed up trial process*	*Response Frequency*	*Response Percentage*
1.	Strongly agree	162	45.00
2.	Agree	48	13.33
3.	Strongly disagree	12	03.33
4.	Disagree	06	01.67
5.	No response	132	36.67
	Total	360	100

210:58.33% of the respondents agree/strongly agree that to speed up the process of trial litigation, one or more of the following just means/measures would be necessary to arrive at just ends, viz.,

- Unless the number of cases is reduced or number of Trial Judges is increased the time required to carry the workload cannot be reduced.
- Judicially work could be done differently by eliminating or reducing certain of its steps, or by being done more intensively, i.e. with fewer diversions during the working and from day to day.
- The Trial Judges might produce more work in a given period, by spending longer or more intensive working hours, or both.
- The solution of the delay problem has to be worked out in terms of elimination of "technicalities", "formalities", "obstructive touts".

The already badly swamped Trial Courts of a general jurisdiction will slowly submerge in a sea of cases or an unmanageable volume of cases, if delay is not handled with resulting effects. 318:88.34% of the respondent's agree/ strongly agree with it.

TABLE 6.36

Sl. No.	Immediate need for delay control with resulting effects	Response Frequency	Response Percentage
1.	Strongly agree	222	61.67
2.	Agree	96	26.67
3.	Strongly disagree	—	—
4.	Disagree	—	—
5.	No response	42	11.66
	Total	360	100

TABLE 6.37

Sl. No.	Non—existence of Relationship between trial Court and law clerk responsible for delay	Response Frequency	Response Percentage
1.	Strongly agree	222	61.67
2.	Agree	96	26.67
3.	Strongly disagree	—	—
4.	Disagree	—	—
5.	No response	42	11.66
	Total	360	100

Unmanageable volume of cases at the Trial Courts happen because of non-existence of a Law Clerk, as already explained above, who can provide the Trial Judges with bright and energetic assistance. 318:88.34% of the respondent's agree/strongly agree with it and they have opined that non-existence of relationship (because of non-availability of a Law Clerk at the Trial Courts) between Trial Court and Law Clerk is mainly responsible for delay at the Trial Court level.

Congestion in the Trial Courts of this country is currently one of the major problem of Judicial Administration and thus congestion of criminal and civil cases has created serious difficulties for the administration of justice, and as such the continued pressure upon existing resources have

TABLE 6.38

Sl. No.	Delay and discouraging unmerited litigation	Response Frequency	Response Percentage
1.	Strongly agree	192	53.34
2.	Agree	72	20.00
3.	Strongly disagree	—	—
4.	Disagree	—	—
5.	No response	96	26.66
	Total	360	100

been such that it is extremely difficult to dispose of cases with promptness and with due regard for just procedures as well as fair trial. What possible and desirable approaches would be the suggestive measures for reducing the heavy amount of cases? 264:73.34% of the respondent's agree/strongly agree that accumulation of cases can be killed if there is case log (record book) as well as lye (cleanser and disinfectant) justification for discouraging unmerited litigation by manipulations. This way loophole in delay may be plugged and riddle of delay may be unknotted.

TABLE 6.39

Sl. No.	Trial Judge vis—à—vis responsibility of a case	Response Frequency	Response Percentage
1.	Strongly agree	204	56.67
2.	Agree	84	23.33
3.	Strongly disagree	06	01.67
4.	Disagree	—	—
5.	No response	66	18.33
	Total	360	100

The basic technique for reduction of delay is simple, viz., A Trial Judge must adopt and apply the philosophy that every case assigned to him becomes his personal responsibility the moment it is filed. It is his duty to push the case to conclusion within the least amount of time reasonable needed for each particular case. 288:80% of the Trial Judges-respondents' agree/strongly agree with it.

TABLE 6.40

Sl. No.	Alternative dispute resolution system	Response Frequency	Response Percentage
1.	Strongly agree	162	45.00
2.	Agree	30	08.33
3.	Strongly disagree	—	—
4.	Disagree	—	—
5.	No response	168	46.67
	Total	360	100

Should alternative mechanism for resolving disputes be appropriate to minimize congestion on the one hand, and lessening delay on the other hand, such as mediation, conciliation, arbitration, inquisitorial process? 192:53.33% Trial Judges-respondents agree/strongly agree that alternative disputes resolution system shall only be workable theorem to resolve the riddle of delay.

7

Budgetary Allocation: Budgetary Problems of Trial Courts

Trial/Lower/Subordinate Court Judges do, in fact, handle the bulk of judicial business under strains of infrastructure facilities as well as court and case management felicitations since the trial/lower/subordinate courts are denied the power of both the sword and purse, and the trial/lower/subordinate courts depend on the mercy as well as cooperation of the coequal branches of government and ultimately public acceptance.[1] Non-financial autonomy may inevitably entail a potential sense of discomfort, frustration, and stultification for the trial court presiding Judges.[2] It has, therefore, been observed that unless the trial judiciary is given full financial autonomy, the problem of pending cases or non-appointment of subordinate/trial court Judges would persist.[3] Be that as it may, it is acknowledged that creating of new posts of trial Judges, increase in the number of trial courts and providing necessary infrastructure and making the courts scientific need finance.[4] It goes further admitted that

1. See, Mark W. Cannon and David M. O'Brien, *op.cit.* at p. 4.
2. *Id.*, p. 50.
3. *The Hindu, Raising The Strength of Judges*, 24.9.2003.
4. *Ibid.*

the judiciary has to petition the Law Ministry each time it needs funds.[5] It is surmising that at present, hardly 0.2% of GNP (or 0.73% of the total revenue) is spent on judiciary in India (when half of this is realized by State Governments through court fees and fines) as compared to other countries such as the U.K., the U.S.A. and Japan where it is between 12 and 15 per cent of the total revenues.[6]

TABLE 7.1

Sl. No.	Increase in appropriation by courts	Response Frequency	Response Percentage
1.	Yes	258	71.67
2.	No	06	01.66
3.	No Comment	96	26.67
	Total	360	100

Trial Judges neither have purse nor sword. And, in such an inhospitable environ it is extremely difficult to manage as a good as well as samaritan manager Trial Courts. Financial autonomy/power to Trial Judges is an extremely ticklish area so for it relates to their judicial function. The Trial Judges do not like to share this problematic area, and it is extremely difficult to comprehend it. Be that as it may, it was desirable to probe into: Should there have been recommendations for increased appropriations for all courts to enable all their needs to be adequately served? 258:71.67% Trial Judges-respondents have affirmatively asserted that there is need for increase in appropriation by Trial Courts to meet their needs that are significantly essential for erasing irritant bottlenecks to improve upon the Trial Court management.

Budgetary allocations vis-à-vis budgetary problems of trial courts depend upon the total receipts in terms of court fees and fines; and annual budget of the trial courts depend

5. *Ibid.*

6. *Ibid.*

TABLE 7.2

Sl. No.	Presiding Officers and Financial Powers	Response Frequency	Response Percentage
1.	Yes	42	11.67
2.	No	108	30.00
3.	No Comment	210	58.33
	Total	360	100

upon expenditure in terms of salary of trial judges, salary of administrative staff, expenditure on administration, and miscellaneous expenditure. Do the Presiding Officers of the Trial Courts have any financial powers on this account? 108:30% Trial Judges-respondents have replied in the negative, and 210:58.33% have no comments to offer and that may be due to the fact that they either do not want to share the truth or they would like to remain escapists or pretentious or non-committal. Be that as it may, the truth at the bottom is that they do not have either the power of the purse or the sword, and they swing between the higher judiciary and the executive. It is but natural that the financial requisitions have to pass through many channels to obtain the requisite sanction prerequisite for the trial courts.

TABLE 7.3

Sl. No.	Determination of staff requirement at Trial Court	Response Frequency	Response Percentage
1.	Officers	—	—
2.	Establishment	—	—
3.	Ministerial	—	—
4.	As per High Court Orders	48	13.33
5.	No response	312	86.67
	Total	360	100

To keep abreast with the increasing workload of the Trial Courts, the need for staff expansion generally is measured on the basis of area, population, crime rate, civil litigation rate, development, and some other factors relating to trial courts infrastructure as well as management. In the backdrop of this, it was imperative to know about the scientific formulae for determining the staff requirement at each level of the Trial Court as it is very much related to financial aspects of the Trial Courts. The responses are not very much encouraging. 48:13.33% only have responded that the staff requirement at each level of the Trial Court is determined as per High Court orders of the respective State, while 312:86.67% have not responded to this variable.

TABLE 7.4

Sl. No.	*Additional Accommodation for Trail Court*	*Response Frequency*	*Response Percentage*
1.	Yes	72	20.00
2.	No	114	31.67
3.	No Comment	174	48.33
	Total	360	100

Some of the Trial Courts in the country are housed in dilapidated buildings that have been declared dangerous for inhabitation; some of the Trial Courts in the country are housed in good buildings; and some of the Trial Courts are housed in moderate buildings. Be that as it may, there is an urgent need for the additional accommodation for the Trial Courts so that they give proper outlook of Justice Houses where the dispensers of justice, friends (Lawyers) of justice, and seekers (clients) of justice feel to work with dignity. In some of the States new buildings of the Trial Courts have been constructed, but the Trial Courts have not been shifted to new buildings for want of dignity space in terms of Lawyers' Chambers in court precincts. Only 72:20% have opined that there seems to be an urgent need for the additional or new accommodation for the Trial Courts in order to ease out the problems of the Trial Courts, while 174:48.33% do not feel so.

The Trial Courts Judges ought to be visionary in court management and that they could reflect through their

TABLE 7.5

Sl. No.	Proposals in the light of future needs and expansion	Response Frequency	Response Percentage
1.	Yes	186	51.67
2.	No	18	05.00
3.	No Comment	156	43.33
	Total	360	100

proposals for future needs and expansion. 186:51.67% of the Trial Judges-respondents do keep the future needs and requirements in mind while submitting the proposals and their economy to the concerned in improving the trial courts environ, while 156:43.33% have no comments to offer and it discerns that such respondents are non-visionaries!

TABLE 7.6

Sl. No.	Use of Modern Technology	Response Frequency	Response Percentage
1.	Yes	12	03.33
2.	No	270	75.00
3.	No Comment	78	21.67
	Total	360	100

Trial Courts' records need to be maintained in scientific manners instead of Stone Age methods of records keeping that attract ants or insects to web their fabric. Has any modern technology been introduced to aid and assist the trial courts' staff to maintain the records scientifically? 270:75% of the respondents have replied in the negative and that may be due to the involvement of heavy purse of the state exchequer.

Responses of the Trial Judges relating to some of the pertinent questions concerning financial position of the Trial Courts have been discouraging, viz., What norms are being adopted for the creation of new Trial Courts at a particular station to clear the back log of cases and to avoid further piling of cases; What norms are being adopted for the creation of Fast Track Courts to reduce huge number of cases pending in the Trial Courts for swift and just disposal; How many Trial Courts are functioning in rented buildings and how many Trial Courts are housed in own buildings; How many Trial Courts have been built up in scientific as well as modern technology giving outlook of court rooms; How many Trial Courts Judges have not been provided with residential accommodations and what is the percentage of such Trial Courts Judges vis-à-vis the total strength; What are the financial powers of Trial Courts Judges; How far the recommendations of the Finance Commissions for providing additional Court buildings, additional amenities for the present Trial Courts buildings and additional residential quarters for Presiding Officers of the Trial Courts for up gradation of judicial administration have been implemented? The responses to these pertinent questions have been in negation. Had the responses been encouraging the inferences could have been altogether different, viz., one could measure budgetary problems as well as financial autonomy of Trial Courts and could offer some suggestive measures for the allocation of budgetary powers and/or financial autonomy, and Trial Courts could be made strong both in purse and sword for the swift and just disposal of cases.

8

Legal Profession Impetus *vis-a-vis* Trial Courts

Relations of the Judiciary with the Public, Press and the Bar

The purpose herein is to understanding sociologically professional behavioural standards and its impetus on the sustainability of trial courts with a view to finding how far the Bench, the Bar, the Public and the Press develop relationship or interaction towards the use of legal action consistent and consonant with and promotional to the societal obligations of the legal profession and the trends of the futurology of the law profession. We expect or aspire perfection from our trial judiciary forgetting that we live in an imperfect world, and the trial court system suffers from some of that imperfection.[1] And, in that imperfection changes and improvements come very slowly.[2] Imperfection at the trial judiciary system inevitably poses certain problems and whatsoever changes and improvements come that must be accepted as Jefferson contended that "half a loaf is better than no bread. If we cannot secure all our rights, let's secure

1. See, Mark W. Cannon and David M. O'Brien, *op. cit.* p. 244.
2. *Ibid.*

what we can".[3] There is no denying the fact that it may be inasmuch as difficult to tread in this area "where the angels would fear to tread" or where it may amount to "making the angels weep".[4] Perhaps, the image is that, "A person who is ignorant of legal matters is always liable to make mistakes when he tries to photograph a court scene with his pen".[5] Sir William Scott contended that, "Courts of Justice do not pretend to furnish cures for all the miseries of human life. They redress or punish gross violations of duty, but they go no further; they cannot make men virtuous; and as the happiness of the world depends upon its virtue, there may be much unhappiness in it which human laws cannot undertake to remove".[6]

Be that as it may, the present study aspires to knowing the attitudes and behavioural approaches of the trial Judges to the legal profession and whether the trial Judges are aware of their social responsibilities. It is, therefore, a study relating to the self-introspection of the trial Judges concerning the social relevance of the profession and its impetus on the working of the trial judiciary including the inefficiency, corruption, and over-crowding, the data would be revealing one. It has been observed that the life of the law is the practice of the law, and in the practice of the law one gets a measure of the extent of protection law affords to the rights, duties and interests of the members of the society; the lawpersons exercise a profound and crucial influence in regulating progress and maintaining order in society under the rule of law.[7] However, there is increasing dissatisfaction with the profession because of delay, exorbitant cost of litigation, and the quality of administration of justice.[8]

---

3. As quoted *op.cit.* at pp. 215-16.
4. *Cf.* Lord Cook of Thorndon, *Where Angels Fear To Tread,* in B.N. Kirpal, *et. al.* (Ed.), Supreme but not Infallible, 2001, p. 97.
5. Mark Twain (1835-1910), *Puddn' head Wilson,* 1894, *A Whisper to the Reason,* quoted in Simon James and Chantal Stebbings (Ed.), A Dictionary of Legal Quotations, 1996, p. 29.
6. *Ibid.*
7. See, Ranjit Mahanty in N.R. Madhava Menon (Ed.), The Legal Profession, 1984.
8. N.R. Madhava Menon, *op.cit.*

Literature on the profession, on the role and the status of the law profession and its impetus vis-à-vis the trial courts is not only scanty, but "largely impressionistic, speculative, and historical".[9] Succinctly, it is with this background cue, an in depth scientific probe has been made about the facts, values and ideologies of the legal profession on the above mentioned probing with the help of heuristic research.

TABLE 8.1

Sl. No.	Conception of legal profession amongst people	Response Frequency	Response Percentage
1.	Yes	204	56.67
2.	No	138	38.33
3.	No Comment	18	05.00
	Total	360	100

The conception of legal profession amongst people of the country varies according to their experiences gained through their encounters with the legal profession and it's working at the Bar and at the corridors of the Justice Temple. The notoriety played with the legal profession by different people is the heart of varied notions about justice delivery system. In the backdrop of this, the respondents were probed in depth to respond to: Is the feeling rampant throughout the people who have to deal with the legal profession, that legal profession is an impediment, roadblock and obstruction to justice because of its dilatory, prolix, technical and formal approach, valid? 204:56.67% Trial Judges-respondents have responded in the affirmative and 138:38.33% have responded otherwise.

One of the primary functions of the legal profession is to assist in rendering justice. But the feeling has generated that the present day profession has moved far from it and its present role is clearly counterproductive. 174:48.33% and 36:10%. Trial Judges-respondents have affirmed the contention

9. *Ibid.;* see also P.V. Kane, History of Dharamsastra, Vol. III, 1993, pp. 242-316.

TABLE 8.2

Sl. No.	*Legal profession and counter productive*	*Response Frequency*	*Response Percentage*
1.	Strongly agree	174	48.33
2.	Agree	36	10.00
3.	Strongly disagree	84	23.33
4.	Disagree	—	—
5.	No response	66	18.34
	Total	360	100

of this variable because they are not pretentious to say otherwise, while 84:23.33% strongly refute the charge and there seems strong pretentious approach to this variable. And, those who refute the proposition, however, have no suggestions to offer to improve the system.

TABLE 8.3

Sl. No.	*Judiciary and legal profession: Confrontationist approach*	*Response Frequency*	*Response Percentage*
1.	Yes	78	21.67
2.	No	234	65.00
3.	No Comment	48	13.33
	Total	360	100

There ought not be any confrontationist approach between the organized profession and the judiciary. Law is an instrument of social engineering. Its two most important limbs are the judiciary and the legal profession and in order to achieving the just goals by just means, their role must be complimentary to each other. A strong feeling has been generated that instead of becoming complimentary, a sort of confrontationist situation has developed between the organized profession and the judiciary. 234:65% of the Trial Judges-respondents do not agree with this proposition, because they still nourish the feelings that the personnel in the noble legal profession are the officers of the courts to assist the judiciary in the rendition of swift and just justice and they are not the explicators of this noble profession devoid of unjust means for achieving unjust ends. However, 78:21.67% have no pretensions or reservations to agree with the proposition. Be that as it may, the truth of the fact remains unrequited that lawpersons in the legal profession are basically responsible for making delay a home in the judicial process and that is the heart of the problem.

TABLE 8.4

Sl. No.	*Strikes by members of legal profession*	*Response Frequency*
1.	Against Professional Ethics	102
2.	Against the interest of the clients	138
3.	Against the cannons of justice	102
4.	Against society	102
5.	Any other, please specify	—
	Total	444

In the backdrop of the above proposition, it was aspired to know from the Trial Judges-respondents how would they assess and evaluate recurrent strike by the members of the legal profession. The legal profession is not a trade nor business nor commerce nor briefs of litigants merchandise, it is a mere intellectual profession. Lawyers' culture to often go on strike, therefore, makes the lawyers, the legal culture, and the professional life-stunning rise to prominence. Due to Lawyers culture of strike, a name unknown and unheard conceptually, there seems to be loss of prestige of the legal profession, and, to some extent, the declining role of the legal profession. Be that as it may, still the professional life survives because of its distinctive culture. Obviously, Lawyers professional behavioural trends, and their self-evaluation tend to unfold the characteristics of the legal milieu, professional norms, and professional ethics. In almost all the Trial Judges-respondents have unequivocally that Lawyers behaviour pattern to go on strike is against professional ethics, interests of the clients, cannons of justice, and society. Justice E.S. Venkataramiah has had the occasion to say *a multo fortiorari* "Who suffers if lawyers, doctors and teachers go on strike? They are the harassed litigants, patients and students. Is it just that these professional men should make them unnecessarily suffered to satisfy their own fancies? These strikes also cause immeasurable injury to the entire community. These strikes are not, therefore, signs of good citizenship."[10] The Supreme Court of India unequivocally *proprio vigore* in *Harish Uppal* v. *Union of India*[11] has opined that Advocates have no right to go on strike or give call of boycott {because such a strike or boycott is neither covered within the ambit of labour legislations nor Code of Civil Procedure nor Code of Criminal Procedure or Indian Advocates Act}. Courts, too, are not required to adjourn cases because lawyers are on strike. Advocates who abstain from attending work in the courts of law due to strike call should be mulcted with costs, and that shall help in preserving the rule of law and upholding the constitutional values. However, protests or abstention from work for one day may be ignored and that too in rarest of rare case.

TABLE 8.5

Sl. No.	*Strikes by legal professionals are against fair play and justice*	*Response Frequency*	*Response Percentage*
1.	Strongly agree	186	51.66
2.	Agree	78	21.67
3.	Strongly disagree	—	—
4.	Disagree	18	05.00
5.	No response	78	21.67
	Total	360	100

10. See and *cf.* the opinion of P.P. Rao, The Bar Council's Strike Call, *The Hindu*, September 2002.

11. A.I.R. 2003 S.C. 739; and see also *Roman Services* v. *Subhash Kapoor*, A.I.R. 2001 S.C. 207; *Supreme Court Bar Association* v. *Union of India*, A.I.R. 1998 S.C. 1895; *Mahabir Prasad Singh* v. *Jacks Aviation Pvt. Ltd.*, A.I.R. 1999 S.C. 287; *K.John Koshy* v. *Dr. Tarakeshwar Prasad Shaw*,(1998) 8 SCC 624; *Communist Party of India (m)* v. *Bharat Kumar*, A.I.R. 1998 S.C. 184; *Indian Council of Legal Aid and Advice* v. *Bar Council of India*, A.I.R. 1995 S.C. 691.

TABLE 8.6

Sl. No.	Propriety of strike by advocates in favour of judiciary against Govt.	Response Frequency	Response Percentage
1.	Yes	114	31.67
2.	No	210	58.33
3.	No Comment	36	10.00
	Total	360	100

The concept of strike is the cessation of work by the employees against the employers as it is a concept of industrial relations. The Lawyers are not the employees of any employer. A strike by the legal profession absenting from the court cannot help in introducing notions of fairplay and justice. 264:73.33% Trial Judges-respondents have affirmed it.

Strike by Lawyers either in their own cause or for and on behalf of a sitting member of the Judiciary who has been unfairly treated by government has no propriety because that may give the impression of seeking favouritism from such member of the Judiciary and that may also affect the independence as well as integrity of the Judiciary on the whole. Therefore, 210:58.33% Trial Judges-respondents have opined that it is not proper for the members of Bar to go on strike in support of their belief that a sitting member of the Judiciary has been unfairly treated by the government, whereas 114:31.67% opine otherwise.

TABLE 8.7

Sl. No.	Strike effecting independence of judiciary in future	Response Frequency	Response Percentage
1.	Yes	240	68.33
2.	No	48	13.33
3.	No Comment	66	18.34
	Total	360	100

Strike by the members of Bar in the long run impairs the independence and reputation of the Judiciary coveted by the Bar. 240:68.33% trial Judges-respondents affirmatively assert it. 66:18.34% of the respondents have no comments to make on this proposition and such of the respondents seem to be in oscillating position.

TABLE 8.8

Sl. No.	*Bar and strike*	*Response Frequency*	*Response Percentage*
1.	Yes	132	36.67
2.	No	216	60.00
3.	No Comment	12	03.33
	Total	360	100

In the backdrop of the above, it is *a multo fortiorari* clear that the Bar cannot and should not go on strike under any circumstances because that leads to merchandising the profession, and as such 216:60% of the respondents have expressed that the Bar and the strike are poles apart from each other. There seems no cause and justification for the Bar to observe strike; strike eventually affects the reputation as well as esteem of the Bar on the whole.

Besides, there seems to be the disinclination of the senior members of the Bar to accept Judgeship of the Trial Courts. The reasons for this are not far to seek. The contemporary legal profession, in a sense, has fallen in the popular estimation, and corruption, money, delay, and falling standards in general, as opined by some of the respondents, are mainly responsible for this saddened state of affairs. What can be done to restore the lost image or reputation or esteem of the legal profession in the country? It seems imperative to introduce some modifications, major or minor, in the existing Advocates Act, and, if possible, the policy conceivers and policy makers may think of bringing new legislation relating to the legal profession in place of the existing one. Besides, disciplinary jurisdiction of the Bar Council of India and State Bar Councils need improvements by providing teeth to them. There is also an impending need to take some measures to curb or contain the alleged hobnobbing and intimacy between the members of the Bar and Judiciary to develop mutual faith and trust as well as synergetic environ.

A feeling has generated that there ought to be association of Lawyers with consumer forums, tribunals and trial courts set up under socially beneficent legislations and to evaluate the vision of the Trial Judges-respondents a probing was deemed to be imperative. How would the Trial Judges evaluate the movement amongst consumers of justice for inclusions of Lawyers in tribunals (such as Consumer Forums) and Trial Courts set up under socially beneficent legislations? And, the Trial Judges-respondents by and large have conceded it a welcome step that is evident from the statistical figures presented in Table 8.9.

TABLE 8.9

Sl. No.	*Evaluation of association of Lawyers in consumer forums*	*Response Frequency*	*Response Percentage*
1.	Useful and good	90	25.00
2.	Not beneficiary	36	10.00
3.	Welcome step	36	10.00
4.	Fair enough	90	25.00
5.	No response	108	30.00
	Total	360	100

There was a time when there used to be tie up between the Lawyers and the politicians; leading Lawyers in the legal profession were deeply involved in the freedom movement of India; legal profession and politics, not politicking, were

TABLE 8.10

Sl. No.	*Necessity for tying up professional bodies*	*Response Frequency*	*Response Percentage*
1.	Yes	306	85.00
2.	No	06	01.67
3.	No Comment	48	13.33
	Total	360	100

TABLE 8.11

Sl. No.	Desirability to have standardized schedule of fees	Response Frequency	Response Percentage
1.	Yes	222	61.67
2.	No	30	08.33
3.	No Comment	108	30.00
	Total	360	100

inseparable as both unlike the present scenario were nobles. In the backdrop of it, it was aspired to know in depth the views of the Trial Judges-respondents to it and as such they were asked to respond to: Is it necessary to prevent a tie up between professional bodies on the one hand and politicians and political parties on the other? 306:85% have responded that there is necessity for tying up professional bodies.

There is a complaint against the legal profession that litigation is costly and that is due to the exorbitant fees being charged by the Lawyers, and as such a pertinent question was asked to the Trial Judges to knowing their views to dispel the impressions about the legal profession. Is it desirable to have a standardized schedule of fees that may be charged from the clients? 222:61.67% respondents have answered in the affirmative though a majority of the respondent 108:30% has responded in the negative. It discerns that there seems to be mixed feeling about it. Those respondents who favour standardized fees schedule do not have any solution as to how should it be arrived at and how would it be enforced?

Besides, the legal profession is monopolized by the seniors and the juniors or new entrants to this noble profession are made to suffer or the juniors are treated as bonded labours because the seniors take best out of the juniors with zero incentives to survive in the profession in the teething trouble/gestation period. It has also been observed that sometimes the seniors make the lives of the juniors' hell thus compelling them to leave the profession in lurch. It has also been observed that sometimes the seniors make use of muscle power compelling the juniors' career at the infancy stage not to bloom as competitors in the profession but leave it in the lurch, and the juniors who have been tread shabbily are intelligent and know their jobs of research as well as presentation before the Bench. Such juniors are not given chance for break through. And, instead of becoming godfather the seniors have proved to be worst than demons. Therefore, what can possibly be done to tone down monopolistic character of professional business? There can't be any straightjacket reply to it, but, nevertheless, it may be possible to think of some norms for distributing caseload among seniors in the Bar and those who are relationally juniors.

Similarly, there is desirability to devise a system by which indigenous litigants must be in a position to appear before Trial Courts on their own and be assisted by voluntary agencies, social action groups and paralegal bodies. This shall reduce contentious adversary process and exorbitant litigation costs as well.

With the spread of terrorism and militancy there seems to be some impetus of it on the legal profession and the functioning of the Trial Courts. The lives of the Lawyers and the Presiding Officers of the Trial Courts are in peril; their private lives are not in peace, and as it is seems to be a severe law and order problem. The specious complaints are being represented to the Human Rights Commissions for the violations of human rights inasmuch as the human rights of the terrorists and militants are dear and near and ajar for the members of the Bar and the Judiciary.

TABLE 8.12

Sl. No.	*Willingness amongst established lawyers to accept judgeship of Trial Court*	*Response Frequency*	*Response Percentage*
1.	Yes	126	35.00
2.	No	234	65.00
3.	No Comment	—	—
	Total	360	100

There is dearth of good Lawyers and judges as well. The Bar and the Bench need to be enriched with good as well as able lawpersons. Whether able lawyers with good and sound practice willing to accept Trial Court Judgeship? 234:65% Trial Judges-respondents, as per their experiences, have replied in the negative, whereas 126:35% have replied in the affirmative.

TABLE 8.13

Sl. No.	*Revised pay scales: an attraction for judgeship*	*Response Frequency*	*Response Percentage*
1.	Yes	258	71.67
2.	No	90	25.00
3.	No Comment	12	03.33
	Total	360	100

Revised emoluments whether sufficiently attractive to accept Trial Courts Judgeship? 258:71.67% Trial Judges-respondents have opined in the affirmative, while 90:25% have opined in the negative.

TABLE 8.14

Sl. No.	*Relevant considerations in appointment of Trial Court judge*	*Response Frequency*	*Response Percentage*
1.	Income	90	25.00
2.	Standing at the bar	216	60.00
3.	Caste	—	—
4.	Reservation principle	—	—
5.	Character integrity etc.	24	06.67
6.	No response	30	08.33
	Total	360	100

What are the relevant considerations/attractions for appointment to trial Courts? Besides character, integrity, caliber and income, the Trial Judges-respondents in majority 216:60% have opined that 'standing at the Bar' seems to be the only relevant consideration/attraction to Trial Courts judgeship.

TABLE 8.15

Sl. No.	Judges and media projection	Response Frequency	Response Percentage
1.	Yes	96	26.67
2.	No	264	73.33
3.	No Comment	—	—
	Total	360	100

Should the Trial Courts stay out of the limelight? A majority of the Trial Judges-respondents 264:73.33% have opined that the Trial Courts should be shy of media projection, because media projection may dispel many specious impressions about the working of the Trial Courts.

General responsibility of the Trial Courts Judges, in the opinions of the majority Trial Judges-respondents, relates to: (i) For safeguarding both rights of the accused and interests of the public in the administration of justice; (ii) Proceedings before the Trial Judge be conducted with unhurried and quiet dignity and should aim at to establish such physical surroundings as are appropriate to the administration of justice; (iii) The trial Judges should conduct the proceedings

TABLE 8.16

Sl. No.	General responsibility of Trial Court judges	Response Frequency
1.	Safeguarding rights of the accused as well as interest of the public	336
2.	Proper and dignified conduction of proceedings	336
3.	Conduction of proceedings in clear and understandable language	336
4.	Professional respect towards the counsels	336
5.	Adherence to court procedure	336
6.	Enhancement of public confidence	336
7.	Avoidance of delay	336
8.	Adherence to working schedule	336
9.	Avoidance of prejudicial approach	336
10.	No response	24

in clear and easily understandable language; (iv) The Trial Judges conduct towards the prosecutors and defense counsels should be such that manifests professional respect, esteem and fairness; (v) The Trial Judges should be familiar with and adhere to the cannons, codes and ethos applicable to the judiciary; (vi) The Trial Judges should reflect the dignity of their offices and enhance public confidence in the administration of justice by their personal appearance and demeanour; (vii) The Trial Judges should have the obligation to avoid delay, continuance and extended recess, except for good cause; (viii) The Trial Judges should be an example in the matters of punctuality, the observance of scheduled court hours, and the use of working tongue; and (ix) The Trial Judges should avoid impropriety, prejudices and the appearance of impropriety in all their activities.

Besides, the Lawyers too could make some positive contributions in the modernization of Trial Courts so that Trial Courts' managerial aspects become improved scientifically that help arrears problem in the Trial Courts is reduced to minimal. They too can help to improve the quality of legal education inasmuch as that it becomes 'legal justice education' so that the Trial Courts get the best of the legal professionalisms to improving the working of the Trial Courts.

It is acknowledged that non-filling up of vacant post of Judges at the higher courts is the major cause for the accumulation of cases and thus the problem of arrears at the superior courts. Similarly, more workload and less number of trial judges at the Trial Courts seems to be chief cause, besides others, that may be attributed for the arrears of cases in crores at the trial Courts level.

TABLE 8.17

Sl. No.	*Importance of role of police in criminal cases*	*Response Frequency*	*Response Percentage*
1.	Yes	336	93.34
2.	No	12	03.33
3.	No Comment	12	03.33
	Total	360	100

Police plays a very vital role in the making or unmaking of a criminal case and in the administration of criminal justice in any democratic nation. 336:93.34% Trial Courts Judges-respondents have not refuted the statement of fact.

TABLE 8.18

Sl. No.	Affectivity in performance of duties of prosecuting officers	Response Frequency	Response Percentage
1.	Satisfactory	181	53.87
2.	Efficient	—	—
3.	Co—operative	40	11.91
4.	Casual	86	25.59
5.	Non co—operative	—	—
6.	Indifferent	—	—
7.	No response	29	08.63
	Total	336	100

In the backdrop of the above, the police authorities/ prosecuting officers appointed in the various courts for the administration of criminal justice discharging their duties, according to the opinions of the Trial Courts Judges, satisfactory (181:53.87%), cooperative (40:11.91%), and casual (86:25.59%).

TABLE 8.19

Sl. No.	Maintenance of police diary by police personnel	Response Frequency	Response Percentage
1.	As per law	90	25.00
2.	Not as per law	216	60.00
3.	Any other	—	—
4.	No response	54	15.00
	Total	360	100

The Police Officers are required to maintain police diary right from the date of investigation to the presentation of chalans in the trial Courts. 216:60% trial Judges-respondents have expressed the police personnel do not maintain police diary as per law, while 90:25% have expressed that they maintain police diary as per law.

TABLE 8.20

Sl. No.	*Satisfactory contribution of police in administration of justice*	*Response Frequency*	*Response Percentage*
1.	Strongly agree	6	01.66
2.	Agree	72	20.00
3.	Strongly disagree	78	21.67
4.	Disagree	126	35.00
5.	No response	78	21.67
	Total	360	100

In the backdrop of the above, according to the experiences of the Presiding Officers of the Trial Courts, the contribution of police in the administration of criminal justice is mixed one, viz., both satisfactory as well as dissatisfactory, and reasons for this are not far to seek.

9

Conclusion

The heuristic study of Trial Courts is a unique study of Trial Courts Management. There is no public/National policy in this perspective, except the keen vision of our Constitution makers to ensure that judiciary—both Superior Courts and Subordinate (Trial) Courts—in India is independent of the Executive.[1] Independence of the Judiciary is ensured when it is allowed to be free from outside influence both from the Executive and the Legislature including the politicians who are the masters of the destiny of democracy. Independence of the Judiciary is the "Basic Structure" of the Constitution of India, for the Judiciary constitutes the foundation on which rests the edifice of our democratic polity.[2] There are no policy guidelines for making an inroad of HRD, the heart of management, in plugging loopholes and streamlining the Trial Courts Management. Well-managed Trial Courts shall be essentially disciplined dispelling all sorts of charges that hamper the systematization of swift and just disposal of cases. It may be conceded that sound management is means to arrive at just ends. Mismanagement of Trial Courts may be

---

1. Art. 50 of the Constitution of India; see Arts. 233-237 of the Constitution of India concerning Subordinate Judiciary.
2. *S.P. Gupta* v. *Union of India,* 1981 Supp. S.C. 87, 408; *Union of India* v. *Bonnerjea* (1995) 6 S.C.C. 765.

suicidal because it may be the fountainhead of "Delays". Mismanagement seems to be the cause of dissatisfaction, for the Managers of Trial Courts turns the noble vocation into vacation. Conversion of noble vocation into vacation may happen due to (i) role of corruption in disposal of cases, (ii) influence of superior judiciary, society, relations, friends and adversaries in the disposal of cases in a particular way, (iii) economic standing of Trial Judges and Advocates, and (iv) beaurocratic and juristocratic behaviour of Trial Judges.

The research study unfolds many mists about the Trial Courts and the Trial Judges, and in its revelation it manifestly and undoubtedly seems that the Trial Courts and the Trial Judges are really on "Trial". The Trial Judiciary is in deep-sea tempest; it has virtually to face many challenges to arrive at the shore creditably; it is grappled with many awesome situations to come out with clean image; it has to encounter/confront many mercenaries bent upon to malign its "Justice Image".

The heuristic data unfold many mysterious aspects of the "first tier" in the judicial system that, in fact, handles the bulk of judicial business. Before referring to what really the heuristic data tell about what goes on at the Trial Courts, it is *sine qua non* to have regard to what indeed is aspired of a Trial Court Judge. Without any inhibition and pretension, the Trial Judges ought to be neutral, detached, kindly, benign, reasonably learned in law, firm but fair, wise, knowledgeable about human behaviour, and somewhat superhuman.

Besides, the qualities in terms of personality of the Trial Judges may be succinctly stated (because none would like to see the reverse of it in a Trial Judge): independence, courtesy and patience, dignity (but not excluding humour), open-mindedness, impartiality, thoroughness and decisiveness, an understanding heart, and social consciousness including his own conscientious aptitude as well as attitude. Be that as it may, a central core of agreed standard defines the Trial Judge as the neutral, impartial, calm, non-contentious umpire standing between the adversary parties, seeing that they observe the rules of the adversary game so that Rule of Law becomes the Rule of Life. The bedrock premise is that the adversary contest is the ideal way to achieve truth and a just result rested upon the truth. In the backdrop of this, the Trial Judge has a more robust part/role, in essence, without caring where the chips may fall. In the quest for truth and righteousness, the Trial Judge ought to be patient, dignified, and courteous to litigants, witnesses, lawyers and others as he presides over the contentious strivings towards that end. Have we succeeded to select the most virtuous or ideal people to adorn the Trial Courts? Is ideal itself very uncertain? Be that as it may, "no judge writes on a wholly clean slate", and as such there is an unhappily wide consensus that excellent Trial Judges are not in long supply. This may be true because it is in the rarest of the rare to find a virtuous or ideal judge, and in the prophetic words of a jurist "a Judge who has not committed any error is yet to be born".[3] It may, however, be conceded that virtues and idealism vary from person to person because of different approach and attitude of counsels, lawyers, prosecutors, defense counsels in the court and Trial Judges behavioural patterns are accordingly oriented.[4] Obviously, the atmosphere of the Trial Courts depends upon the attitudes and approaches the counsels of their clients present in the Trial Courts. Justice Felix Frankfurter has opined it: "Judges are men, not disembodied spirits. Of course, a Judge is not free from preferences or, if you will, biases".[5] The Supreme Court of India has had the occasion to rightly sound in *K.P.Tiwari* v. *State of M.P.*[6]:

> . . . The lower judicial officers mostly work under a charged atmosphere and are constantly under a psychological pressure with all the contestants and

---

3. See Justice Shetty Commission Report, *op. cit.*
4. *Id.*, p. 1.
5. Justice Felix Frankfurter, Nature of Judicial Process of Supreme Court Litigation, 98 Proceedings AM Phil Society, 233 (1954); Benjamin N. Cordozo, The Nature of Judicial Process, pp. 168-69.
6. (1994) Supp. 1 SCC 540; see also *Braj Kishore Thakur* v. *Union of India* (1997) 4SCC 65, 66, 70; *A.M. Mathur* v. *Pramod Kumar Gupta* (1990) 2 SCC 533, 539; *State of Rajasthan* v. *Prakash Chand* (1998) 1 SCC 1; *R.C. Sood* v. *High Court of Judicature at Rajasthan*, A.I.R. 1999 S.C. 707.

> their lawyers almost breathing down their necks—more correctly up to their nostrils. They do not have the benefit of a detached atmosphere of the higher courts to think coolly and decide patiently. Every error, however, gross it may look, should not, therefore, be attributed to improper motive.

In the backdrop of this, the Trial Judges do deserve considerable actions and reactions in deeds, words, and expressions from within as well as outside devoid of open criticism, and intemperate language. The Trial Judges too have to be receptive to enhance as well as enliven their dignity, honour, independence shorn of "contempt of court shield" to cover their deeds and misdeeds.

The sociological survey on "Trial Courts Trial..." reveals the multifaceted story of Trial Courts Judges and Trial Courts. The sociological survey has been conducted on some theoretical hypotheses that unfold many hidden secrets of Trial Courts, Trial Courts Judges, their behavioural trends, strategies and futurology vision plans about Trial Courts and Law Profession.

Tables 2.1 to 2.34 tell about the Profile—Socio-Economic-Educational—of the Trial Courts Judges. The presentation of the background characteristic of the Trial Courts Judges is *sine qua non* as the data on this parameter bear direct relation to need gratification and occupational attitudes of the Trial Courts Judges adorning the Trial Judiciary which is an important independent impartial segment in the hierarchy of the judicial institutions that is conceived to dispense justice devoid of *Raga, Lobha, Bhaya, Dvesha, and Vadinoscha*. Justice is a sword, which requires no scabbard. Hence, it is imperative to have a social audit of Trial Courts Judges who have an intimate correlation with law, justice and profession. A close study of the background characteristics of Trial Courts Judges unfolds many aspects of the personality of Trial Judges. The background characteristics of Trial Courts Judges are certainly potent for predicting courtroom crafts and courtroom results. The data on the background characteristics is potent to correlate with behavicural perspectives, viz., on testing relations between their characteristics and their decision-making propensities. And, that is the revelation of the data on the profile of the Trial Courts Judges.

Tables 3.1 to 3.16 significantly relate to attitude and aptitude of Trial Courts Judges to be Trial Courts Judges. As a Lower (Trial) Court Judge, he decides cases in accordance with what he finds the law to be, and rarely or occasionally he may make clear what he thinks it ought to be. Succinctly, attitudes and aptitudes have relationships with motivation, temperaments, likes, dislikes and idiosyncrasies having impetus in the decision-making process.

Tables 4.1 to 4.17 are significant because correlation between job satisfaction and infrastructure facilities ultimately culminate into efficiency in the decision-making process at the trial level. Therefore, data on this parameter assist to establish correlations between job satisfaction and the trends of efficiency in the job output which is no doctrinaire treatment but which stands close to actual life. Therefore, Trial Courts Judges ought to be expressive in this perspective. Those who are casual to the profession or indifferent to the profession or mock to the profession may remain dissatisfied throughout, and it has been observed that in some cases such lawpersons have never written any singular landmark judgment in their whole career except granting adjournments. In order to increase efficiency in court work output it is *sine qua non* on the government (s) to provide modern electronic facilities to the Trial Courts Judges, as per Justice Shetty Commission Report, and the Trial Courts have been provided with computers, etc. facilities. However, computers should not be used as sophisticated typewriters for court work output, but they must be utilized to the optimum with regard to internet, intra and inter linkage, connections with Higher Courts, E-conferencing, etc. in order to have quick disposal of cases to unloading the Trial Courts with case-load in millions and trillions. Be that as it may, in some places visited by the researcher it has been observed that the computers have been kept unattended to thus making way for the dust to pile on computers, or due to dearth of computer trained personnel the computers have been kept unused in most of the Trial Courts in the country. However, it has been interesting to note that in Pune, Bombay, Andeman and Nikobar Islands the Trial Courts have been well equipped with the computers with optimum as well as excellent use. Though computers have been provided in the most difficult terrain area of Leh and Ladakh but kept unused.

It is the general feeling that the generalist approach to the disposal of cases is the basic cause of delay, because the application of the mind of the Trial Judge from one trend setting to another trend setting consumes time. It is difficult to pin point towards a particular cause for delay. Though Advocates are heart of the problem of delay, but it is not one cause but multiplicity of causes are the roots for delay in the disposal of cases, such as cumulatively judges, Advocates, litigants, legal proceedings all are responsible causes of delay.

Tables 5.1 to 5.45 relate to Court Management. Court Management is a juristic technique as well as art. Court management does not mean to bureaucratize the judicial system and make it to be known as "juristocratic" institution. Court management and case management are correlated to maximize efficiency and minimize deficiency. Court management and case management seem to be the sole soul of judicial process devoid of juristocratic recidivist deviance in decision-making process. The general concept of court management is that the cases at the trial level are managed in such a way that cases at trial level are disposed of swiftly and justly. Court management and case management are just means to arrive at just ends. Court management and case management have varied dimensions that require the induction of new technologies of training to the Trial judges either at the induction level or periodical refresher or continuing legal education courses to update their knowledge with techniques of fast track disposal. The technological developments and information technology as well as computers culminate in enhanced efficiency, productivity and quality. As such, inclusion of Information Technology Action Plan in judicial administration of Trial (Subordinate) Courts in India shall be conducive to enhance operational efficiency, productivity and quality in justice delivery system. It shall improve efficiency, coordination, accessibility and speed in the judicial administration and court as well as case management. It shall minimize bottlenecks, delays, arrears and backlogs. It shall help to develop sound judicial management information system, case management and file management, and Docket management in the Trial Courts. It shall ease out the Trial Courts from an antiquated atmosphere/system. Therefore, there is a fast track need to overhaul the Trial Courts lest they become bankrupt. The data presented on different parameters in this perspective unfold many mists/mystiques. Time management revelation is worth mentioning. Time management and court management are correlative and unless and until both go hand in hand with each other there ought to be friction and irritant results. A single minute lost eventually affects the case-rate disposal. No single minute should be wasted at the cost of courtrooms timings as well as litigant's timings.

Tables 6.1 to 6.40 relate to Delay. Attitudes, Habits, Tenure, Filing of cases may be conceded to be the units of measurements for delay. The data presented unfold many untold stories about the mysteries of delay in the disposal of cases. The general concept is that the cases at the trial level are managed in such a way that cases are disposed of swiftly and justly with least bottlenecks. But, the Trial Judges function under strains, handicaps, hapless conditions, caseload crisis, and as such there appears to be delay. There is the impression that juristocratic recidivism deviance attitude of lawpersons may be the causal factor for delay and the Trial Judiciary has been misunderstood.

There is also a complaint that instead of Trial judges managing the cases, the lawyers have purloined the court and case management, and, hence, delay. Court and case management problems are grave and great and are due to, there is nothing pretentious about it, the mutation in the character of cases since the civil and criminal litigation have evolved into complex proceedings, full of adversaries, interstices, pre-trial problems, discoveries, allegiance to indecisiveness and disinterestedness and culminating in lengthening trial as well as delay in disposal of cases. During research, the research team has come across a typical case of delay; namely, there was an arbitration award in 1993 that was accepted by all the persons to the award. The arbitrator award was presented in the High Court of the jurisdiction for registration and making it a rule of the law of the court. In the later part of the same year, one beneficiary of the award filed a case in the District Court that the arbitration award should not be implemented since his signatures to the award were forged one. Since 1993 till date the District Court has not been in a position to decide whether the signatures of the said beneficiary-petitioner are genuine or false. This is the notoriety in the judicial process for the concurrence of delay where litigants, Advocates of the litigants, Trial Courts Judges, and the legal procedures cumulatively are responsible causes of delay. Hence, delay is a riddle wrapped in mystery inside an enigma.

It has also been seen that Trial Courts Judges are unable to cope with the torrent of cases and to handle such torrent of cases they have to be virtuous because that defines their qualities in terms of personality that may be ineluctable. Be that as it may, there is some tension as well as inconsistency between the professed ideals and the realities with the result that delay in the disposal of cases occur with the piling of cases in the trial/lower courts. It is being felt that piling of cases may yield death knell of the judicial system; it is also a fact that creating workload now changes the very nature of Trial Courts, "threatening to convert them from deliberative institutions to processing institutions, from a judiciary to a bureaucracy. ... However, efficient the judicial branch may become, it cannot mass-produce justice. Wise decisions cannot be made if cases come in vast numbers on judicial assembly line".[7]

It is evident that delay in disposal of cases is due to (a) pending of 23.9 million cases in India's 12822 courts (12800 Subordinate/Trial/Lower Courts, 21 High Courts and 1 Supreme Court), (b) endless adjournments and other sluggish ways of delaying justice, (c) corrupt judiciary and judicial officers, and (d) shortage of judges.

In the backdrop of this, it is not *ipse dixit* but realistically to ease the Trial Courts from the contagious

7. Alvin B. Rubin, *op.cit.*

disease of delays, the felt need to revamp the trial judiciary is to weed out the deadwood and the corrupt and corruption from the corridors of the lower judiciary and to reinvest the trial judiciary with virtuous and quality trial judges.

It also discerns from the data that the felt necessity is to remove snags in raising the strength of the trial/lower courts judges to dispense justice swiftly, fairly and justly. It has been inferred that one of our biggest worries is that paucity of judges in law courts in general and the subordinate/lower/trial courts in particular is the main cause for unconscionable delays in the disposal of cases and consequent build-up of arrears. Therefore, the felt need for increasing the strength of trial judges (proportionately to population and proportionate to population of cases) is to wipe out the mounting arrears and also minimizing or ameliorating delay.

Besides, the trial judiciary has suffered utter neglect be it be in matters of reforms, infrastructure, manpower, management, timely appointment of judges, timely filling of vacancies, provision for basic facilities to enable subordinate/trial/lower courts to function at reasonable level of efficiency.

Besides, the individual habits, too, play a subtle role in the building of a personality of a trial judge as a dispenser of justice. Habits develop a judicious thinking process, justice mind, justice perceptions, justice vision, and cumulatively culminating into justice delivery system. Habits and personality go hand in hand to make a trial judge a great jurist, he may not be a mere pen pusher but the producer of great decisions, and as such a trial judge must have time to think, to ponder, to read and to write meaningfully.

Tables 7.1 to 7.6 narrate the story of/about "Budgetary Allocation *vis-a-vis* Budgetary Problems of Trial Courts". The inferences of the statistical data on the said parameters are that the trial courts are denied the power of both the sword and purse.

The trial courts in the country do not have the privilege of financial autonomy and they depend on the mercy as well as cooperation of the coequal branches of the government. Non-financial autonomy may necessarily entail a potential sense of discomfort, frustration, stultification, and mounting as well as piling of arrears leading to death knells of trial judiciary. It is acknowledged fact that increase in the number of trial judges and trial courts, providing necessary infrastructure and making the trial courts scientific need finance. On the whole, it discerns that the trial courts at present have to remain satisfied with 0.2 of GNP (or 0.73% of the total revenue). What a paradox dismal!

The statistical data enjoined in Tables 8.1 to 8.20 address to "Legal Profession Impetus vis-à-vis Trial Courts: Relations of Judiciary with the Public, Press and the Bar" that is imperative in the policy perspectives of the Trial Courts Management when Trial Courts are put on trial. The heuristic data enjoin herein lead to understanding sociologically professional behavioural standards and its impetus on the sustainability of trial courts with a view to finding how far the Bench, the Bar, the Public and the Press develop relationship or interaction towards the use of legal action consistent and consonant with and promotional to the societal obligations of the legal profession and the trends of the futurology of the law profession. The data presented in these Tables relate to the self-introspection of the Trial Courts Judges concerning the social relevance of the profession and its impetus on the working of the trial judiciary including the inefficiency, corruption, increasing dissatisfaction with the profession because of delay, exorbitant cost of litigation, lack of adequate/propitious/salubrious management, and the quality of administration of justice.

The heuristic study of Trial Courts Trial: Trial Courts Management aspire perfection from our Trial/Lower/ Subordinate Judiciary forgetting that we live in an imperfect system, and the Trial Courts system is no exception to imperfection. Be that as it may, in that imperfection changes and improvements come very slowly. It has been seen that imperfection at the Trial Judiciary system inevitably poses certain problems and whatever changes and improvements come that must be accepted as Jefferson has had contended that "half a loaf is better than no bread. If we cannot secure all our rights, let's secure what we can".[8] It has been awful to

8. *Op.cit.*

tread in this area endeavoring to photograph a court scene with researcher's pen "where the angels would fear to tread"[9], or may amount to "making the angels weep".[10] Succinctly, could it be virtuous to conclude that there seems to be much unhappiness in the Trial Courts Management, which human laws cannot undertake to remove.

9. *Op.cit*
10. *Op.cit.*

QUESTIONNAIRE

PROFILE OF THE TRIAL COURT JUDGE: SOCIAL-ECONOMIC-EDUCATIONAL BACKGROUND

1.1. Name:
1.2. Date of birth:
1.3. Age (in years):
1.4. Religion:
- ❑ Hindu
- ❑ Muslim
- ❑ Christian
- ❑ Parsi
- ❑ Any other

1.5. Caste:
- ❑ Brabmin
- ❑ Kashtriya
- ❑ Vaishya
- ❑ S.C./S.T./O.B.C.
- ❑ Sunni
- ❑ Shia
- ❑ Catholic
- ❑ Protestants
- ❑ Any other, please specify

1.6. Area:
- ❑ Urban
- ❑ Rural

1.7. Mother tongue:
1.8. Marital Status:
- ❑ Married
- ❑ Umnarried
- ❑ Divorcee
- ❑ Any other, please specify

1.9. Number of dependants:
1.10. Present occupational status:
- (i) Lawyer
- (ii) Munsiff
- (iii) Sub-Judge
- (iv) C.J.M.
- (v) City Judge Junior Division
- (vi) City Judge Senior Division

(vii) Sessions Judge/Additional Sessions Judge/Ist Additional Sessions Judge/llnd Additional Sessions Judge/IIIrd Additional Sessions Judge.
(vii) District and Sessions Judge.
(ix) Principal District Judge.
(x) District Judge/Additional District Judge/Ist Additional District Judge/find Additional District Judge/IIIrd Additional District Judge.
(xi) Matrimonial Judge
(xii) T.A.D.A. Court Judge
(xiii) Municipal Magistrate
(xiv) Any other, please specify

1.11. Educational qualifications:
(a) Baccalaurate: B.A./B.Sc./B.Com.
Year: Class & %age:
(b) Masters: M.A./M.Sc./M.Com.
Year: Class & %age
(c) Legal: LL.B./LL.M./LL.D.
Year University Class/%age Nature of LL.B. 2 years/3 years/5 years.
(d) Any other, please specify

1.12. Monthly income:
(i) Rs. 0-5000
(ii) Rs. 5001-10000
(iii) Rs. 10001-15000
(iv) Rs. 15001-20000
(v) Rs. 20001-25000
(vi) Rs. 25000 and above (Please specify)

1.13. Educational qualifications of your parents:

Father *Mother*

(i) Illiterate
(ii) Under matric
(iii) Matric
(iv) Under-graduate
(v) Graduate
(vi) Post-graduate
(vii) Law Graduate
(viii) Technical (B.E./MBBS/Others, Please specify)

(ix) Any other, please specify

1.14. Occupational status of your parents:

Father *Mother*

(i) Business, please specify
(ii) Civil Service, please specify
(iii) Defence, please specify
(iv) Lawyer (Years of standing)
(v) House wife/unemployed
(vi) Teacher (School/College/ University/Technical Institution/ Professional Institution)
(vii) Worker: Skilled/unskilled
(viii) Judge: Subordinate Court/ High Court/Supreme Court/ Tribunal Court ( )
(ix) Any other, please specify

1.15. Monthly income of your parents:

Father *Mother* *Both*

(i) Upto Rs. 1000
(ii) Rs. 1001-2000
(iii) Rs. 2001-3000
(iv) Rs. 3001-4000
(v) Rs. 4001-5000
(vi) Rs. 5001-6000
(vii) Rs. 6001-7000
(viii) Rs. 7001-8000
(ix) Rs. 8001-9000
(x) Rs. 9001-10000
(xi) Rs. 10001 and above (Please specify)

2.1. What was your pre-Trial Court Judge Career Pattern?

(a) Advocate:
Date of Joining Bar
Place of Practice
Muffasil
Urban (Distruct Head quarter)
A.P.O. or P.O.
Number of years standing

(b) Whole time Law teacher:
University Department
Law College (University)

Date of Joining
Date of Leaving
Total number of years
(c) Part time Law Teacher:
University Department
Law College (University)
Date of Joining
Date of Leaving
Total number of years
(d) Any other (in addition to experience at Bar) Please specify:

2.2 What were you Pre-Trial Court Judge (a) political affiliations?
(i) Indian National Congress
(ii) Bhartiya Janata Party
(iii) C.P.I.
(iv) C.P.M.
(v) Samata Party
(vi) J.D.(U)
(vii) Local Regional Party (Please specify)

2.3. Do you continue to follow the same (a) political ideology? ***Yes/No***

2.4. (a) Were/are your parents (father/mother/both) follow the same (a) political party ideology to which you follow? ***Yes/No***
(b) If No, please specify the nature of their (a) political ideology.
(i) Indian National Congress
(ii) B.J.P.
(iii) C.P.I
(iv) C.P.M.
(v) Samata Party
(vi) J.D.(U)
(vii) Local Regional Political Party (Please specify)
(viii) Any other, please specify.

3.1. When were you appointed as a Trial Court Judge?
Date of appointment
Age at time of appointment

3.2. What was the method of recruitment?
(i) State Public Service Commission

(ii) Selection Board through written test and oral interview constituted by the State High Court.
(iii) Selection Board through written test and oral interview constituted by the State Government.
(iv) Any other, please specify.

3.3. Who has been the appointing authority?
(i) State Governor
(ii) Chief Justice of the State High Court
(iii) Any other, please specify

3.4. Please specify the nature/process/method of eligibility and recruitment:
(a) Experience:
Bar: Actual practice for atleast 1/2/3/4/5 yrs.
Other:
(b) Quota for recruitment:
(i) Direct recruitment : %age
(ii) Open merit : %age
(iii) Selection from the members of the Bar : %age
(iv) Selection from the members of S.C./S.T./O.B.C. : %age
(c) Method:
(i) Written exams
(ii) Oral (viva-voce)
(iii) Both
(d) Language requirement: ***Yes/No***
(e) Emergency recruitment: Retired Trial Judges may be appointed: ***Yes/No***
(f) Age of recruitment:
Not less than:
Not more than:
(g) Minimum Educational Qualification to be recruited as a Trial Court Judge:
(h) Disqualification to be a Trial Judge:
Bigamy/conviction/misconduct/any other
(i) Agency for recruitment:
(i) High Court
(ii) State Public Service Commission
(iii) State Govt. (Deptt. of Law/General)
(iv) State Judicial Services
(j) Representation of other bodies and their process:

(i) Chief Justice of a High Court or a Judge of the High Court Deputed by the Chief Justice of the High Court.
(ii) Two Judges of the High Court nominated by the Chief Justice.
(iii) Chief Secretary of the State
(iv) A secretary of a Law Secretary nominated by the Governor/Lt. General.
(v) A Committee of the Judges constituted by Chief Justice of High Court
(vi) Any other, please specify:

3.5. What is your total number of years experience as a Trial Court Judge?

3.6. What shall be yours date and age of retirement as a Trial Court Judge?

3.7. (a) Do you expect a promotion in your career? *Yes/No*

3.7. (b) If yes, what should be the pattern?
(i) Merit alone
(ii) Caste/Community/Regional identification
(iii) Political
(iv) Any other, please specify

3.8. (a) What is the date if your retirement?

3.8. (b) What Post-retirement position do you expect?
(i)
(ii)
(iii)

4.1. What is the nature/structure of Trial Courts in your State?
High Court
Trial Courts (Subordinate Courts)
Principal District and Sessions Judge
Additional District and Sessions Judge
Senior Subordinate Judge
Junior Sub Judge
Munsiffs ètc.
Please Specify:

4.2. Please specify the distance of place of your residence Trial Court:
(i) Less than 1 Km

(ii) 1-2 Kms
(iii) 2-4 Kms
(iv) 4-6 Kms
(v) 6 and above, please specify

4.3. How do you come to Court?
(i) Own scooter
(ii) Own car
(iii) Official car
(iv) Public transport (Please specify)
(v) Taxi/Autorikshaw
(vi) On foot

ATTITUDE AND APTITUDE TO BE A TRIAL COURT JUDGE

5.1. (A) In which year and from which University did you complete your Law Degree (LL.B.)?

Year *University* *Nature of LLB. De!ree*
(a) 2 years
(b) 3 years
(c) 5 years

5.1. (b) What class or division and percentage of marks did you obtain in LL.B.?

5.1. (c) Did you pursue LL.M. studies? ***Yes/No.***

5.1. (d) If yes, please specify the name of the University and year of completion of LL.M.

5.1. (e) Did you pursue doctorate in Law (Ph.D./LL.D.)? ***Yes/No***

5.1. (f) If yes, please specify the name of the University and year of completion of doctorate degree in Law.

5.2. (a) In which year did you procure practising Licence from the Bar Council of India?

5.2. (b) For how many years did you practise at the Bar before joining as a Trial Court Judge?

5.3. In which year and what place did you join as a Presiding Officer of the Trial Court?

Date *Place*

5.4 (a) Did you intend to be a lawyer when you joined LL.B. study course in the University Law Department/Law College affiliated to the

University where from you obtained you LL.B. Degree? *Yes/No*

5.4 (b) Did you intend to be a Judge at the Trial Court when you joined LL.B. study course or when you joined legal practice at the Bar?

(i) Joined LL.B. *Yes/No.*
(ii) Practice at the Bar *Yes/No.*
(iii) Both *Yes/No.*

5.4 (c) If yes to (a) and (b), who decided legal career for you?

(i) You yourself
(ii) Your parents
(iii) Friends (Law/Non-law)
(iv) Teacher
(v) Drifted

5.4 (d) As a legal career, presiding officer of the Trial Court has been your:

(i) First choice ( )
(ii) Second choice ( )
(iii) Third choice ( )

5.4 (e) Are there other (father/guardian) Lawyers or Judges (Trial Court/High Court/Supreme Court) in your family? *Yes/No.*

5.4 (f) If yes, have they been a source of inspiration to you to take up legal career? *Yes/No*

5.5 (a) Did you consider other alternatives of your career? *Yes/No*

5.5 (b) If answer is in affirmative, what alternative career did you decide on?

(i) To be a Doctor
(ii) To be an Engineer
(iii) To be a Scientist
(iv) To be in Banking Service
(v) To be a School/College/University teacher in the subject of ________________
(vi) To be an I.A.S./I.P.S./I.F.S. State Administration service through State P.S.C.
(vii) To be in Defence Service (Officer Rank/ Ordinary rank)
(viii) To be in Judge Advocate General Branch (Army/Air Force/Navy)

(ix) To be a Labour Welfare Officer
(x) To be a personnel Officer
(xi) To be an Administration Officer in Private/Public/Multinational concern.
(xii) Any other, please specify.

5.6. In case you decided an alternative career for you, these why did you choose legal career for you?
(i) Made an attempt in competitive examination, but could not qualify in a competitive examination.
(ii) Could not get admission anywhere in the country in the institutions imparting higher/technical/professional/MBA/MCA examination.
(iii) Any other, please specify.

5.7 (a) Did you compete for any of the following examinations in the past?
(i) I.A.S./I.P.S./I.F.S. ***Yes/No***
(ii) State Administration/Police Service through State P.S.C. ***Yes/No***
(iii) Banking ***Yes/No***
(iv) Defence ***Yes/No***
(v) Any other, pl. specify ***Yes/No***

5.7. (b) Did you get through the written part of any of the above exams? ***Yes/No***

5.7. (c) If yes, were you finally selected for any appointment for any of the above posts? ***Yes/No***

JOB SATISFACTION AND INFRASTRUCTURE FACILITIES

6.1. Do you have job satisfaction as well as security as a Trial Court Judge? ***Yes/No***

6.2. Do you live in:
(i) Own house
(ii) Rented accommodation
(iii) Govt. allotted accommodation
(iv) Any other, please specify

6.3. (a) Have you availed L.T.C./Home Town L.T.C. facility to spend some leisure time and recreation with your family? ***Yes/No***

6.3. (b) What has been frequency of such facility availed by you?

(i) Very frequent
(ii) Frequent
(iii) Occasionally
(iv) Rarely

6.3. (c) Whether medical facility has been allowed to:

(a) (i) Self *Yes/No*
(ii) Family *Yes/No*
(b) (i) Self and dependents *Yes/No*
(ii) Family and dependents *Yes/No*

6.3. (d) What is the frequency of medical facility availed by you?

(i) Very frequently
(ii) Frequently
(iii) Occassionally
(iv) Rarely
(v) Never

6.3. (e) Whether such medical facility is with certain limit? *Yes/No*

6.3. (f) If the answer to the above question is in affirmative, what sorts of the limitations out of the following is imposed?

(i) Specification as to doctor *Yes/No*
(ii) Pecuniary/monetary limitations
As to medical reimbursement *Yes/No*
(iii) Fixed medical reimbursement *Yes/No*
(iv) Any other, please specify:

6.4 (a) Do you have the following facilities at your home at government or self expenses?

(i) Telephone *Yes/No* Govt./Self
(ii) Computer *Yes/No* Govt./Self
(iii) Fax *Yes/No* Govt./Self
(iv) Word processor *Yes/No* Govt./Self
(v) Electronic Typewriter *Yes/No* Govt./Self
(vi) Mnual Typewriter *Yes/No* Govt./Self
(vii) Law Library *Yes/No* Govt./Self

6.4 (b) Do you have the following facilities at your Trial Court Office at Government expenses?

(i) Telephone *Yes/No*
(ii) Computer *Yes/No*
(iii) Fax *Yes/No*

(iv) Word processor *Yes/No*
(v) Electronic Typewriter *Yes/No*
(vi) Manual typewriter *Yes/No*
(vii) Law Library *Yes/No*
(viii) Court Room with retirement room *Yes/No*
(ix) Witness Boxes *Yes/No*
(x) Adequate furniture *Yes/No*

6.4 (c) Whether adequate staff has been made available to you in the nature of:

(i) Steno *Yes/No*
(ii) Reader *Yes/No*
(iii) Clerk *Yes/No*
(iv) Peon *Yes/No*
(v) Case-caller *Yes/No*
(vi) Nazar *Yes/No*
(vii) Piyada *Yes/No*
(viii) Process server *Yes/No*

NATURE OF CASES ASSIGNED

7.1 The nature of cases you are assigned to try as a presiding officer of the Trial Court:

(i) Civil Suits *Yes/No*
(ii) Criminal cases *Yes/No*
(iii) Civil and Criminal both *Yes/No*
(iv) Family/Matrimonial case (Hindu, Muslim, Christian and Parsi) *Yes/No*
(v) Anti Corruption cases *Yes/No*
(vi) Rent cases (Shops and Houses) *Yes/No*
(vii) Municipal cases *Yes/No*
(viii) Excise cases *Yes/No*
(ix) Electricity cases *Yes/No*
(x) Forest cases *Yes/No*
(xi) Traffic cases *Yes/No*
(xii) Bank cases *Yes/No*
(xiii) Patent/copy right *Yes/No*
(xiv) T.A.D.A. Cases *Yes/No*
(xv) Land dispute *Yes/No*
(xvi) Cinematography *Yes/No*
(xvii) Registration of variety of deeds *Yes/No*

(xviii) Succession certifications *Yes/No*
(xix) Consumer cases *Yes/No*
(xx) Motor Accident Cases *Yes/No*
(xxi) Any other please specify:

7.2 (h) What is the basic cause of delay in disposal of cases:
(i) Due to the Judges
(ii) Due to the Advocates
(iii) Due to litigant
(iv) Due to legal procedures/Loop holes
(v) if any other : please specify

7.2. (i) Do you agree that the generalist approach to the disposal of cases is the basic cause of delay, because the application of the mind of the Trial Judge from one trend setting to another trend setting consumes time? ***Yes/No***

7.3 Do you agree that the structure of Trial Courts is segregated/separated as exhaustive that the nature of cases for disposal can be easily segregated/separated and the specialized Trial Judges with expertise specialization in the nature of cases can be engaged for the quick disposal of cases? ***Yes/No***

7.4. Do you agree with the submissions of the governments (at the Centre and the States) that the structure of the Trial Courts cannot be separated as it would be against the existing legal system and it shall create a financial problem? ***Yes/No***

7.5. (a) Recently, there have been emerging "changing perceptions of Law in India" and as such lawmen are attempting to determine the extent to which modern law notions have penetrated the village and the degree of congruence between the value premises of the new legality and those of customary practice. Do you agrce with the statement. ***Yes/No***

7.5. (b) If yes, should it be an appropriate approach to a better understanding of the confrontation between traditional law ways and the modern law to investigate village client? ***Yes/No***

7.5 (c) If answer to 7.5(b) is in affirmative then a

systematic description of litigants in District and Munsiff Courts would yield important information on the role of Law in Indian modernization. ***Yes/No***

7.5 (d) Who comes to the town Courts from the village?
- (i) Zamindars/Landlords
- (ii) Land-holders
- (iii) Tillers of the soil
- (iv) Poor to seeking matrimonial maintenance
- (v) Peasants against village money lenders
- (vi) Money-lenders against peasants
- (vii) Any other, please specify.

7.5. (e) What does the villager hope to achieve by involving himself with the modern Courts?
- (i) Justice
- (ii) Quick Justice
- (in) Simple procedure
- (iv) Avoid technicalities of law
- (v) Uncorrupt
- (vi) Any other, please specify

7.5 (f) Is the adversary process previewed as a modality for realizing justice? ***Yes/No***

7.5 (g) (I) What images of the modern law-givers are carried back to the village?
- (i) Independence of the Trial Courts
- (ii) Integrity of the Trial Judge
- (iii) Impartiality of the Trial Judge
- (iv) Clean image of the Trial Judge
- (v) Corrupt image of the Trial Judge

7.5 (g) (II) "Is Judicial Administration faulty and face value favourtism of some judges of Subordinate Judiciary/Lawyers is another cause of denial of justice? ***Yes/No***
- (i) Is Court staff also responsible for it? ***Yes/No***
- (ii) Is non-effectiveness of Judges responsible for it? ***Yes/No***

The questions 7.5(h) to 7.5(k) can be approached either from the perspective of the professionals who transmit the modern legal culture—the judicial administrations and legal practitioners—or of those who may receive it—the clients."

7.5 (h) How shall we investigate the impact of the legal system on the Indian populace?

7.5 (i) How widely disseminated are the Trial Courts decisions and how well observed and enforced are the rules embodied in them?

7.5 (j) Can the Courts and lawyers help to inculcate beliefs and habits of political behaviour appropriate to constitutionalism?

7.5. (k) What is being taught about the "role of law"' by whom and to whom?

COURT MANAGEMENT

8.1. What are the components of Trial Office?

(i) Office Clerk 1/2/3/4/------
(ii) Office Steno 1/2/---------
(iii) Office peon 1/2/3----------
(iv) Case caller 1/2/-----------
(v) Any other (Please specify)

8.2. How Trial Court office is maintained?

8.3 (a) When does the office staff reach the Court?

(i) 8 a.m.
(ii) 9 a.m.
(iii) 10 a.m.

8.3 (b) When does the office staff leave the court?

(i) 1.30 p.m.
(ii) 2 p.m.
(iii) 3 p.m.
(iv) 4 p.m.
(v) 5 p.m.
(vi) 6 p.m.

8.4 (a) When does the Trial Judge reach the court office?

(i) 8 a.m.
(ii) 9 a.m.
(iii) 10 a.m.
(iv) 11 a.m.
(v)

8.4 (b) When does the Trial Judge leave the court?

(i) 1.30 p.m.
(ii) 2 p.m.

(iii) 3 p.m.
(iv) 4 p.m.
(v) 5 p.m.
(vi) 6 p.m.

8.4 (c) What are the Trial Court timing?
(i) 8 a.m. to 2 p.m.
(ii) 9 a.m. to 5 p.m.
(iii) 10 a.m. to 5 p.m.
(iv) 10 p.m. to 5.30 p.m.

8.4 (d) After arriving at Court Office, how much time does the Trial Judge take to come to Court Room from his court office to start trial proceedings?
(i) <15 minutes
(ii) 15-20 minutes
(iii) 20-25 minutes
(iv) 25-30 minutes
(v) 30> minutes

8.4 (e) When does the Trial Judge leave the court room for court office attached to the court room?
1. Any time during the proceedings of the case.
2. Only at lunch time: 1 p.m. to 2 p.m.

8.4 (f) Does the Trial Judge leave the court room in post-lunch session for the break? ***Yes/No***

8.4 (g) If yes, for how long?
(i) for 15 minutes
(ii) for half an hour

8.4 (h) When does the Trial Judge close the court proceedings in post lunch session?
(i) No proceedings are conducted in post lunch session.
(ii) At 3 p.m.
(iii) At 4 p.m.
(iv) At 5 p.m.

8.4 (i) Alter the close of the court proceedings, does the Trial Judge spend time in his court office to study cases? ***Yes/No***

8.4 (j) If yes, how much time does he spend in the court office?
(i) < one hour

(ii) 1-2 hours
(iii) 2-3 hours
(iv) 3-4 hours
(v) 4 > hours

8.4 (k) After the close of the court proceedings, does the Trial Judge spend time in his court office to write judgements of the finally heard cases? *Yes/No*

8.4 (l) If yes, how much time does he spend in the court office for the purpose?
(i) < 1 hour
(ii) 1-2 hours
(iii) 2-3 hours
(iv) 3-4 hours
(v) 4 > hours

8.6 (a) Is the Trial Court adequately/sufficiently equipped with infrastructure facilities of modern scientific gazettes to handle the proceedings efficiently?
(i) Steno *Yes/No*
(ii) Computer *Yes/No*
(iii) Internet *Yes/No*
(iv) E-mail *Yes/No*
(v) Fax *Yes/No*
(vi) Word processer *Yes/No*
(vii) Electronic typewriter *Yes/No*
(viii) Any other, please specify

8.6 (b) Whether the court office staff is adequately trained to handle the above electronic gazettes? *Yes/No*

8.6 (c) In case the office staff is adequately trained, are there provisions for their upgradation in service career? *Yes/No*

8.6 (d) If answer to the above is in negative, does it mean the irresponsibility of the government thus creating disinterest in the office staff? *Yes/No*

8.6 (e) What is the attitude of the office staff towards the presiding officer of the Trial Court?
(i) Respectful and helping
(ii) Respectful but not helping
(iii) Helping
(iv) Indifferent

(v) Only working relation
(vi) Compromising
(vii) Uncompromising
(viii) Unhelpful
(ix) Any other, please specify.

8.6 (f) What is the profile of the office staff?

	Clerk	*Steno*	*Non-Clerical*
(i) Religion			
(ii) Caste			
(iii) Educational Qualification			
(iv) Area			

8.6 (g) Whether services of scientific gazettes are made thereself to the complainant/clients? ***Yes/No***

8.6 (h) Is the library of the Trial Court well equipped with law literary? ***Yes/No***

8.6 (i) If yes, the quantum and the nature of books and Law reports available:
(i) Number of books and law reports
(ii) Nature of books
(iii) Nature of law reports

8.7 (a) Whether attached bathroom/toilet facilities are made available to the Trial Judge? ***Yes/No***

8.7 (b) Whether separate bath room/toilet facilities are made available to the advocates in the court-room precincts? ***Yes/No***

8.7 (c) Whether common bathroom/toilet facilities are made available to the advocates and the visitors in the court-room precincts? ***Yes/No***

8.7 (d) Whether separate bathroom/toilet facilities are made available to the female advocates and female visitors in the court-room? ***Yes/No***

8.8 (a) What is the time interval between the cases filed/accepted in the Court Office and taken-up for trial process?
(i) < a week
(ii) one to two weeks
(iii) two to three weeks
(iv) three to four weeks
(v) four to five weeks
(vi) five and > weeks (please specify)

8.8 (b) Do you agree that unreasonable gap of time interval between the acceptance of the case in the court office and taken up for trial process is the basis/foundation for the delay in the disposal of cases? ***Yes/No***

8.9 (a) Once the trial process is over, the papers have to be prepared by the court office, how much time the court office consumes in preparing the papers to be placed before the Trial Judge for finally writing the judgement? (Time Gastae)

(i) < a week
(ii) one to two weeks
(iii) two to three weeks
(iv) three to four weeks
(v) four to five weeks
(vi) five and> weeks (please specify)

8.9. (b) This time gastae may be conceded the cause of:

(i) Influence by the parties
(ii) Corruption of office staff by the parties
(iii) Any other, please specify

8.10 (a) Is the trial procedure complicated? ***Yes/No***

8.10 (b) If yes, what causes could be attributed for it?

(i)
(ii)
(iii)

8.10 (c) What measures do you feel are conducive to simplify the trial procedure so that the trial process consumes less time for the disposal of cases/complaints?

(i)
(ii)
(iii)
(iv)
(v)
(vi)

8.11 (a) What is the frequency of transfer of Court office Staff?

(i) 1/2/3/4/5/6 ——> years

8.11 (b) What is the frequency of transfer of Trial Court Judge?

(i) 1/2/3/4/5/6 ——> years

8.12. "The distribution of the work load or systematization of the work load is the backbone of court management and is determined by the number of working units available with the Trial Court Judges."

(i) Strongly agree
(ii) Agree
(iii) Strongly disagree
(iv) Disagree
(v) Can't say

8.13. "In order to make the trial judicial process swift and just, a fresh approach to judicial administration by promoting court reforms through improvements in general administration is inevitable".

(i) Strongly agree
(ii) Agree
(iii) Strongly disagree
(iv) Disagree
(v) Can't say

8.14. "Statistics of backlog and fresh cases indicate that existing administrative procedures as well as practices of all Trial Courts are not adequate to cope with ever growing case loads and as such many litigants are faced with intolerable delay."

(i) Strongly agree
(ii) Agree
(iii) Strongly disagree
(iv) Disagree
(v) Can't say

8.15. In keeping with traditional concepts of an independent judiciary the Trial Courts have been left largely to their own devices to solve administrative problems and to initiate the reforms. But the Trial Courts have not taken enough initiations to solve their own problems, and as such the Parliamentarians as well as the State legislature's have been indifferent to the few proposals for reforms that have been brought forth.

(i) Strongly agree
(ii) Agree
(iii) Strongly disagree

(iv) Disagree
(v) Can't say

8.16. The experiences indicate that adding more Trial Judges/creating Fast track Courts can at times be no solution at all.
(i) Strongly agree
(ii) Agree
(iii) Strongly disagree
(iv) Disagree
(v) Can't say

8.17. It should not be concluded pre-maturely that Trial Courts are incapable of serving as a forum for peaceful settlement of disputes in an increasingly complex world.
(i) Strongly agree
(ii) Agree
(iii) Strongly disagree
(iv) Disagree
(v) Can't say

8.18. To overcome the problem of congestion and delay three important steps in Court Management/Administration must be taken.
(a) Each Trial Court system must have a Supervisory Judge with the power and personnel to make and implement administration devices.
(b) Each Trial Court system must establish procedure to collect and analyze detailed current information about all relevant aspects of the Court's operations.
(c) Each Trial Court system must have adequate facilities, competent clerical personnel, and office procedures that promote the efficient administration of justice for sound Judicial ManagementlAdministration.
(i) Strongly agree
(ii) Agree
(iii) Strongly disagree
(iv) Disagree
(v) Can't say

8.19. Thus far, most Trial Judges have been reluctant to make use of the services of Management consultants

This is in part due to the lawyers traditional distrust of methods that are new and strange.

(i) Strongly agree
(ii) Agree
(iii) Strongly disagree
(iv) Disagree
(v) Can't say

8.20. The Management Consultants themselves have not made their usefulness clear to the Judiciary. They have failed to explain in cogent terms just what their studies can accomplish. They have failed to assuage the fear of the Legal Fraternity that "efficiency experts" will be unable to distinguish between delays in the Trial Judicial process that serves the ends of Justice and delays that are unnecessary and avoidable by improved management.

(i) Strongly agree
(ii) Agree
(iii) Strongly disagree
(iv) Disagree
(v) Can't say

8.21. The Trial Courts and the consultants have to recognize each other's needs and potentialities, they can co-operate to make the Trial Judicial System a modern instrument of Justice.

(i) Strongly agree
(ii) Agree
(iii) Strongly disagree
(iv) Disagree
(v) Can't say

8.22. The Trial Courts control over the trial calendar should be vested in the Trial Court Judge.

(i) Strongly agree
(ii) Agree
(iii) Strongly disagree
(iv) Disagree
(v) Can't say

8.23. The lawyers should support the authority of the Court and the dignity of the Trial Court Room by strict adherence to the rules of decorum and by manifesting an attitude of professional respect toward the Trial Judge, opposing Counsel, witnesses, defendants, and others in the Court Room.

(i) Strongly agree
(ii) Agree
(iii) Strongly disagree
(iv) Disagree
(v) Can't say

8.24. The heart of the Judicial process is the trial. The trial is based essentially in an adversary system of procedure. Although the Trial Courts in dense centres of population are plagued with ever mounting case loads, deteriorating physical facilities, insufficient, inefficient time spend—thrifters personnel no Trial Courts anywhere in the country compare in importance with them from the standpoint of inculcating confidence in the Judicial system for vast numbers of our citizens.

(i) Strongly agree
(ii) Agree
(iii) Strongly disagree
(iv) Disagree
(v) Can't say

8.25. There is a necessity to provide Judicial manpower. A sufficient, competent as well as efficient number of Trial Judges should be provided for each Judicial District to assure for the prompt and fair administration of justice.

(i) Strongly agree
(ii) Agree
(iii) Strongly disagree
(iv) Disagree
(v) Can't say

8.26. There is impending need of adequacy of court room facilities and supporting staff. The Trial Judge should be provided with court facilities which are dignified and functional to assure the prompt and fair administration of justice.

(i) Strongly agree
(ii) Agree
(iii) Strongly disagree

(iv) Disagree
(v) Can't say

8.27. In order to obtain the objections set forth in question 8.26, the Trial Judge has an obligation to seek the co-operation of the executive and legislative departments to provide Judicial manpower, supporting staff, physical facilities, and adequate budget.
(i) Strongly agree
(ii) Agree
(iii) Strongly disagree
(iv) Disagree
(v) Can't say

8.28. In order to attain the above mentioned objectives, the Trial Judge should be familiar with the nature and extent of the inherent power of the Judiciary to compel other agencies of government to provide for staff, facilities and funds.
(i) Strongly agree
(ii) Agree
(iii) Strongly disagree
(iv) Disagree
(v) Can't say

8.29. The Trial Judge has the duty to have the Court staff properly trained/under effective control?
(i) Strongly agree
(ii) Agree
(iii) Strongly disagree
(iv) Disagree
(v) Can't say.

8.30. The Trial Judge has a duty to see that the reporter makes a true, complete and accurate record of all proceedings with professional independence.
(i) Strongly agree
(ii) Agree
(iii) Strongly disagree
(iv) Disagree
(v) Can't say

8.31. The Trial Court Judge has the ultimate responsibility for the docket, i.e. for proper management of calendar in criminal cases and civil suits.

(i) Strongly agree
(ii) Agree
(iii) Strongly disagree
(iv) Disagree
(v) Can't say

8.32. The Trial Court Judge should make known before trial that no colloquy, argument or diseussions take place directly between counsels in the presence of the Trial Court Judge.
(i) Strongly agree
(ii) Agree
(iii) Strongly disagree
(iv) Disagree
(v) Can't say

DELAY: ATTITUDES, HABITS, TENURE, FILING OF CASES ETC., (UNIT OF MEASUREMENT)

9.1. Since how long you as a Judge has been occupying the position in this Trial Court?
1/2/3/4/5/6/7/8/9/10 -------- years.

9.2 (a) When do you get up in the morning?
(i) 4 a.m.
(ii) 4.30 a.m.
(iii) 5 a.m.
(iv) 5.30 a.m.
(v) 6 a.m.
(vi) 6.30 a.m.
(vii) 7 a.m.

9.2 (b) Do you go for morning walk?
Yes/No/Spending leisure time
Timings..................................

9.2 (c) Do you go for evening walk after you come back from Court Office? *Yes/No/Spending leisure time*
Timings..................................

9.2 (d) In whose company do you prefer to go for mornings and evenings walk?
(i) Alone
(ii) With wife
(iii) With wife and children

(iv) With lacunae (Lawyers, brethren/fellow trial judges)
(v) With non-lacunae (Please specify)
(vi) With friends: Law Professionals/Non-Law Professionals)

9.2 (e) Do you meditate in the morning and evenings? *Yes/No*
Timings...............................

9.2 (f) At what time do you retire for bed?
(i) 8 a.m.
(ii) 9 a.m.
(iii) 10 a.m.
(iv) 11 a.m.
(v) 12 midmght

9.2 (g) Do you read the news paper(s) daily? *Yes/No*

9.2 (h) If yes, which newspaper do you read? *Local/National*

9.2 (i) Do you prefer to read central editorial, views and articles page? *Yes/No*

9.2 (j) If yes, do you enjoy reading the central page? *Yes/No*

9.2 (k) Do you watch T.V.? *Yes/No*

9.2. (l) If yes, what is your favourite T.V. Channel?
(i)
(ii)
(iii)
(iv)
(v)
(vi)
(vii)
(viii)

9.2 (m) What programmes do you prefer to watch on T.V.?

(i) News	National/Local/Both (Language: Hindi/English/Both/Local)
(ii) Serials	Please specify (Language: Hindi/English/Both/Local)
(iii) Movies	Please specify

(Language: Hindi/English/Both/Local)

(iv) Shastriyya sangeet Please specify:

(v) Geetmala (filmi songs) (Language: Hindi/English/Both/Local)

(vi) Any other, please specify:

9.3 (a) (i) Is in service Refresher Course in Law/Orientation Course in Law/Continuing Legal Education training through National Judicial Academy or State Judicial Academy imparted to the Trial Court Judges to keep them abreast with modern developments of Law? *Yes/No*

9.3 (a) (ii) Will imparting of Judicial training to clerical staff for judicial work improve judicial system? *Yes/No*

9.3 (b) If yes, have they ever attended such a course? *Yes/No*

9.3 (c) If yes, how many times under your total span of judicial career?

(i) One Place
(ii) Two Place
(iii) Three Place
(iv) Four Place
(v) Name

9.3 (d) What is the frequency of such a training?

(i) Once a year
(ii) After every 2 years

9.3 (e) In which language, such training course is conducted?

(i) Hindi
(ii) English
(iii) Local ( )
(iv) Both Hindi and English
(v) Both Local ( ) and English

9.4. Do you agree that a provision for the attachment of a Court clerk (who shall always be a fresh law graduate in 1st class from the Law College/Law Schools/Law Department/Law University with the Trial Judge would essentially help the Trial Judge in swift and efficacious disposal of class? *Yes/No*

9.5 (a) How many total number of cases pending in your Trial Court?
(i) Civil
(ii) Criminal
(iii) Matrimonial
(iv) Miscellaneous: Please specify

9.5 (c) What is the disposal rate of cases?
(i) Daily
(ii) Weekly
(iii) Monthly
(iv) Yearly

9.5 (d) Whether rate of disposal of cases in your opinion, is satisfactory?
(i) Satisfactory
(ii) Above average
(iii) Average
(iv) Unsatisfactory

9.5 (e) With the rate of disposal, are the arrears/ accumulation of cases:
(i) Increasing Why
(ii) Decreasing Why

9.5 (f) What, in your opinion, is the Judge: case ratio?
(i)
(ii)
(iii)
(iv)
(v)

9.5 (g) What, in your opinion, is the present Judge: population ratio?
(i)
(ii)
(iii)
(iv)

9.5 (h) What, in your opinion, should be the Judge: population ratio?
(i)
(ii)
(iii)
(iv)

9.5 (i) What in your opinion, should be Judge:rate

disposal ratio?

(i)
(ii)
(iii)
(iv)

9.7 (a) (i) Is accumulation/piling of cases

(i) Encouraged
(ii) Discouraged

9.7 (a) (ii) Are effective steps necessary to overcome this problem of accumulating/piling of cases.

9.7 (b) What steps are taken to keep the people aware about the accumulation of cases?

(i) Educating the mind of the people through reporting in the press. Local/National
(ii)
(iii)

9.8 Hearing and disposal rate in pre-lunch session is swifter and just as compared to post lunch session.

(i) Strongly agree
(ii) Agree
(iii) Strongly disagree
(iv) Disagree
(v) No opinion.

9.9 (a) Do you agree that Mandays lost due to frequent holidays (National/State/Local) contribute to the piling of cases as well as delay in the disposal of cases? *Yes/No*

9.9 (b) Do you agree that to minimize piling of cases as well as delay, more Mandays should be increased by curtailing holidays? *Yes/No*

9.9 (c) Please give you suggestions to decrease holidays and increase Mandays:

(i)
(ii)
(iii)
(iv)

9.10. Delay can be termed as a fountainhead of indecisiveness and indecisiveness causes unpleasantness.

(i) Strongly agree

(ii) Agree
(iii) Strongly disagree
(iv) Disagree
(v) No opinion

9.11. What could be the fountain head cause of delay?
(i) Inadequate manpower
(ii) Inefficient manpower
(iii) Incompetitor manpower
(iv) Frequent adjournments just on demand.

9.12. Do you agree that delay in Trial Courts has become almost entirely identified with the problem of two many cases/suits flowing from the original parent case/suit and too many appeals? ***Yes/No***

9.13. Do you agree that the problem of delay can be eliminated if the problem of too many cases/suits from the parent cases/suits and too many appeals is solved by increasing the number of trial judges? ***Yes/No***

9.14. Delay in Court process continues because the trial process of litigation is accusatorial and, because, is time consuming. The total work load of Trial Court is determined by the number of cases that have to be handled, multiplied by average amount of work that has to be performed in connection with each case.
(i) Strongly agree
(ii) Agree
(iii) Strongly disagree
(iv) Disagree
(v) No opinion

9.15. To speed up the process of trial litigation, one or more of the following measures would be necessary:
(a) Unless the number of cases is reduced or number of Trial Judges is increased the time required to carry the work load cannot be reduced.
(b) Judicially work could be done differently by eliminating or reducing certain of its steps, or by being done more intensively, i.e. with fewer diversions during the working and from day to day.
(c) The Trial Judges might produce more work in a given period, by spending longer or more intensive working hours, or both.

(d) The solution of the delay problem has to be worked out in terms of elimination of "technicalities" "formalisms" "obstructive touts".
   (i) Strongly agree
   (ii) Agree
   (iii) Strongly disagree
   (iv) Disagree
   (v) No opinion

9.16. The already badly swamped Trial Courts of a general jurisdiction will slowly submerge in a sea of cases or an unmanageable volume of cases, if delay is not handled with resulting effects.
   (i) Strongly agree
   (ii) Agree
   (iii) Strongly disagree
   (iv) Disagree
   (v) No opinion

9.17. Unmanageable volume of cases at the Trial Courts happen because of non-existence of a Law-clerk (the Law clerks are graduates fresh from Law Schools stand at the top of their classes) who can provide the Trial Judges with bright, energetic assistance.
   (i) Strongly agree
   (ii) Agree
   (iii) Strongly disagree
   (iv) Disagree
   (v) No opinion.

9.18. Accumulation of cases can be killed if there is case log (record book) as well as lye (cleanser and disinfectant) justification for discouraging unmerited litigation by manipulations.
   (i) Strongly agree
   (ii) Agree
   (iii) Strongly disagree
   (iv) Disagree
   (v) No opinion

9.19 Congestion in the Trial Courts of this country is currently one of the major problem of Judicial Administration and thus congestion of criminal and civil cases has created serious difficulties for the administration of justice, and as such the continued pressure upon existing resources have been such that is it extremely difficult to dispose of cases with promptness and with due regard for just procedures as well as fair trial. What possible and desirable approaches do you suggest for reducing the heavy amount of cases?

(i)
(ii)
(iii)
(iv)
(v)

9.20. 1. Should alternative mechanism for resolving disputes be appropriate to minimize congestion such as mediation. conciliation, arbitration, inquisitorial process?

(i) Strongly agree
(ii) Agree
(iii) Strongly disagree
(iv) Disagree
(v) No opinion

9.20. 2. The basic technique for reduction of delay is simple: A Trial Judge must adopt and apply the philosophy that every case assigned to him becomes his personal responsibility the moment it is filed. It is his duty top push the case to conclusion within the least amount of time reasonable needed for each particular case.

(i) Strongly agree
(ii) Agree
(iii) Strongly disagree
(iv) Disagree
(v) No opinion

BUDGETARY ALLOCATION: BUDGETARY PROBLEMS OF TRIAL COURTS

10.1 Should there have been recommendations for increased appropriations for all courts to enable all their needs to be adequately served? *Yes/No*

10.2. What are the total receipts of the Trial Court during the last ten years:

	Year	*Court Fees*	*Fines*
1.	1990		
2.	1991		
3.	1992		
4.	1993		
5.	1994		
6.	1995		
7.	1996		
8.	1997		
9.	1998		
10.	1999		
11.	2000		
12.	2001		

10.3. What is the break-up of the annual budget of the Trial Court in terms of expenditure during the last the years?

	Year	*Annual Budget*	*Salary of Trial Judges*	*Salary of Staff*	*Expenditure on ADM*	*Misc. Expd.*
1.	1990					
2.	1991					
3.	1992					
4.	1993					
5.	1994					
6.	1995					
7.	1996					
8.	1997					
9.	1998					
10.	1999					
11.	2000					
12.	2001					

10.4 (a) Do the Presiding Officers of the Trial Courts have any financial powers? ***Yes/No***

10.4 (b) If yes, to what extent?

10.4 (c) If no, through how many levels channels the requisition has to pass to obtain the requisite sanction?

(i)

(ii)

(iii)
(iv)
(v)
(vi)

10.5 (a) What is the prescribed present staff strength of the Trial Courts.

10.5 (b) To keep abrcast with the increasing workload of the Trial Courts.

(i) On what basis is the need for staff expansion considered?
(i)
(ii)
(iii)
(iv)
(v)

(ii) Is there any scientific formula for determining the staff requirement at each level of the Trial Court?
(i) Officers
(ii) Establishment
(iiii) Ministerial

(iii) Is any thought given to the need for the additional accommodation for the Trial Court?
(i)
(ii)
(iii)

(iv) Are the future needs and expansions kept in mind while submitting the proposals?

(v) How are Trial Courts records maintained?

(vi) Has any modern technology been introduced to aid and assist the staff to maintain records?

(vii) What are norms, if any, being adopted for the creation of a new Trial Court at a particular station?

(viii) What are norms being adopted for the creation of Fast Track Courts?

(ix) Are you satisfied with such norms, if not what in your opinion should be such norms.

(x) What is the total number of Trial Courts in the State and how many such Courts are functioning in rented buildings?

(xi) How many Trial Courts Judges have not been provided with residential accommodation and what is the percentage of such Trial Courts Judges vis-a-vis the total strength?

(xii) What are the financial powers of the Trial Judge?

(xiii) How far the recommendations of the Finance Commissions (8th) for providing additional Court buildings, additional amenities for the present Court buildings and additional quarters for presiding officers for upgradation of Judicial administration have been implemented?

LEGAL PROFESSION IMPETUS *VIS-A-VIS* TRIAL COURTS: RELATIONS OF THE JUDICIARY WITH THE PUBLIC, PRESS AND THE BAR

11.1 Is the feeling rampant throughout the people who have to deal with the legal profession, that legal profession is an impediment, roadblock and obstruction to justice because of its dilatory, prolix; technical and formal approach, valid? *Yes/No*

11.2. One of the primary function of the legal profession is to assist in rendering justice. But the feeling has generated that the present day profession has moved far from it and its present role is clearly counterproductive.

(i) Strongly agree
(i) Agree
(iii) Strongly disagree
(iv) Disagree
(v) No opinion.

11.2 (a) If you strongly agree or agree with the above mentioned proposition kindly suggest how to improve the system.

11.3 (a) Law is an instrument of social engineering. Its_two most important limbs are the Judiciary and the legal profession and in order to achieving the goals, their role must be complimentary to each other. Is it true that instead of becoming complimentary, a sort of a confrontationist situation has developed between the organized profession and the Judiciary? ***Yes/No***

11.3 (b) If the answer to the above is in the negative, how would you assess and evaluate recurrent strike by the legal profession?

(i) Against professional ethics
(ii) Against the interests of the clients.
(iii) Against the canons of justice
(iv) Against society
(v) Any other, please specify

11.3 (c) The concept of strike is the cessation of work by the employees against the employers as it is a concept of industrial relations. The lawyers are not the employees of any employer. A strike by the legal profession absenting from the court cannot help in introducing notices of fairplay and justice.

(i) Strongly agree
(ii) Agree
(iii) Strongly disagree
(iv) Disagree
(v) No opinion

11.3 (d) Is it proper for the members of Bar to go on strike in support of their belief that a sitting member of the Judicially has been unfairly treated by Govermnent. ***Yes/No***

11.3 (e) Would it in the long run impair the independence of the Judiciary coveted by the Bar? ***Yes/No***

11.3 (f) Can the Bar go on strike? ***Yes/No***

11.3 (g) If yes, for what cause and with what justification?

(i)
(ii)
(iii)
(iv)
(v)

12.1. How would you view the disinclination of the senior members of the Bar to accept Judgeship of the Trial Courts?

(i)
(ii)

(iii)
(iv)
(v)

12.2 (a) In what sense, the contemporary legal profession has fallen in the popular estimation?
(i)
(ii)
(iii)
(iv)
(v)

12.2. How would you evaluate the movement amongst consumers of justice for inclusions of lawyers in tribunals (Such as Consumer Forums) and Trial Courts set up under socially beneficent legislations?
(i)
(ii)
(iii)
(iv)
(v)

12.2 (b) What can be done to restore the lost image or esteem of the legal profession in the country?
(i) Some modifications, minor or major, in the existing Advocates Act.
(ii) New Act to replace the present Advocates Act.
(iii) Disciplinary Jurisdiction of the Bar Council of India and State Bar Councils needs improvement, such as:
(a)
(b)
(c)
(d)
(e)
(f)
(iv) Suggestive general outlines of the New Advocates Act:
(a)
(b)
(c)
(d)
(e)
(f)

12.3. What measures may be taken to curb or contain the alleged hobnobbing and intimacy between:

(i) The members of the Bar and Judiciary:

(a) To develop mutual faith and trust

(b)

(c)

(d)

(ii) The Members of the Bar and prosecuting Officers:

(a)

(b)

(c)

(d)

(e)

12.5 Is it necessary to prevent a tie-up between professional bodies on the one hand and politicians and political parties on the other? ***Yes/No***

12.6 (a) Is it desirable to have a standardized schedule of fees that may be charged from the clients? ***Yes/No***

12.6 (b) If yes, how should itbe arrived at?

(i)

(ii)

(iii)

(iv)

12.6 (c) How would it be enforced? ***Yes/No***

12.7 (a) What can possibly be done to tone down monopolistic character of professional business?

(i) It is possible to think of some norms for distributing case load among seniors in the Bar and those who are relationally juniors.

(ii)

(iii)

12.7 (b) Is it opportune to devise a system by which indigenous litigants must be in a position to appear before Trial Courts on their own and be assisted by voluntary agencies, social action groups and para-legal bodies? ***Yes/No***

12.7. (c) What is the impetus of terrorism, militancy on the legal profession and the functioning of the Trial Courts?

(i)

(ii)
(iii)
(iv)
(v)

12.8 (a) Whether able lawyers with good and sound practice willing to accept Trial Court Judgeship? *Yes/No*

12.8 (b) Revised emoluments whether sufficiently attractive to accept Trial Court Judgeship? *Yes/No*

12.8 (c) What are the relevant considerations for appointment to Trial Courts:

(i) Income *Yes/No*
(ii) Standing at the Bar *Yes/No*
(iii) Caste *Yes/No*
(iv) Reservation principle *Yes/No*
(v) Non-reservation principle character, integrity, caliber taken into account. *Yes/No*

12.8 (d) Should the Trial Courts stay out of the limelight? *Yes/No*

12.8 (e) General responsibility of the Trial Court Judge relates to:

(i) For safeguarding both the rights of the accused and interests of the public in the administration of jusce. *Yes/No*
(ii) Proceedings before the Trial Judge be conducted with unhurried and quiet dignity and should aim at to establish such physical surroundings as are appropriate to the administration of justice. *Yes/No*
(iii) The Trial Judges who should conduct the proceedings in clear and easily understandable language. *Yes/No*
(iv) The Trial Judges conduct towards the prosecutors and defer counsels which should manifest professional respect, esteem and fair. *Yes/No*
(v) The Trial Judges who should be familiar with and adhere to the cannons and codes applicable to the judiciary. *Yes/No*

(vi) The Trial Judges who should reflect the dignity of their office and enhance public confidence in the administration of justice by his personal appearance and demeanour. *Yes/No*

(vii) The Trial Judge should have the obligation to avoid delay, continuance and extended recesses, except for good cause. *Yes/No*

(viii) The Trial Judge who should be an example in the matters of punctuality, the observance of schedule Court hours, and the use of working tongue. *Yes/No*

(ix) The Trial Judge who should avoid impropriety, prejudices and the appearance of impropriety in all his activities. *Yes/No*

13.1 (a) What contributions lawyers can make in the modernization of Trial Courts?

(i)
(ii)
(iii)
(iv)
(v)

13.1 (b) What role lawyers can play in the modernization of the legal system that the arrears problem in the Trial Courts is reduced to minimal?

(i)
(ii)
(iii)
(iv)
(v)

13.1 (c) What contribution lawyers can make in the modernization of the Indian Legal Education so that the Trial Courts get the best of the legal professionists to improving the working of the Trial Courts?

(i)
(ii)
(iii)

(iv)
(v)

13.1 (d) It is acknowledged that the non-filling up of vacant post of Judges at the higher courts is the major cause for the accumulation of cases and thus the problem of arrears at superior court. What Chief causes could you attribute for the arrears of cases in crores at Trial courts level?

(i)
(ii)
(iii)
(iv)
(v)

14.1 (a) "Police plays a very vital role in the making or unmaking of a criminal case and in administration of criminal justice in any democratic nation". Do you agree with this proposition? ***Yes/No.***

14.1 (b) If yes, are the Police Authorities/Prosecuting Officers appointed in the various courts for the administration of criminal justice discharging their duties.

(i) Satisfactorily
(ii) Efficiently
(iii) Co-opertive
(iv) Casually
(v) Non co-operative
(vi) Indifferent

14.1 (c) According to your experience do the Police authorities/personnel maintain the Police Diary?

(i) As per Law
(ii) Not as per Law
(iii) Any other, please specify

14.1 (d) According to your experience, explain whether the police authorities contribution in the administration of Justice is satisfactory.

(i) Strongly agree
(ii) Agree

(iii) Strongly disagree
(iv) Disagree
(v) No opinion

14.1 (e) If you strongly disagree or disagree what means can be effective?
Please specify:

Bibliography

Abraham, Henry J., The Judicial Process, 1986.

B. Sheintag, The Personality of the Judge, New York, 1944.

Basu, Durga Das, Constitution of India, 1999.

Brownlie, Ian, *et. al.* Basic Documents on Human Rights, 2003.

C. Wyzanski, A Trial Judge's Freedom and Responsibility, 65 Harvard Law Rev., 1281 (1952).

Canon, Mark W. and O'brien, David M., Views from the Bench, 1987.

Communiast Party of India (M) *v.* Bharat Kumar, A.I.R. 1998 S.C. 184.

Desai, Ashok A. Justice *versus* Justice, 2000.

Duncun, J. and Derret, M. History of Indian Law, 1973.

Francis Bacon, Essays, 1625.

Government of India, The First National Judicial Pay Commission Report, Justice Jagannath Shetty, 2002.

Harish Uppal *v.* Union of India, A.I.R. 2003 S.C. 739.

Harold Koontz, *et. al.*, Essentials of Management,1982

Hogg, Peter, Constitutional Law of Canada, 2003.

Indian Council of Legal aid and Advice *v.* Bar Council of India, A.I.R. 1995 S.C. 691.

Judge Ms. Fern M., Smith Educating the Judiciary, Span, Jan.-Feb. 2001.

Julius Stone, Social Dimensions of Law and Justice, 1999.

K. John Koshy *v.* Dr. Tarakeshwan Prasad Shaw (1998) 8 SCC 624.

K.L. Bhatia, *et. al.*, Delay A Riddle Wrapped in Mystery Inside An Enigma, 1996 J.I.L.I.

Kirpal, B.N., *et. al.*, Supreme but not Infallible, 2000.

Krishnaswamy, P., Justice V.R. Krishna Iyer—A Living Legend, 2000.

Law Commission of India, 1. 121 Report: A New Forum for Judicial Appointments, 1987.

Lord Justice Woolf, Report on Access to Justice, 1996.

M. Frankel, The Search for Truth: An Umperial View, 123 University of Pennsylvania ,Law Rev. 1031 (1975).

M. Rosenberg, The Qualities of Justices—Are they Sustainable, 44 Texas Law Rev. 1966.

M.A. Khan and Mrs. Dalvi, Court Management and Case Management, (Unpublished 1997)

M.P. Jain, Outlines of Indian Legal History, 1981.

Mahabir Prasad Singh *v.* Jacks Aviation Pvt. Ltd., A.I.R. 1999 S.C. 287.

Moghe, S.G., History of Dharmsastra—In Essence, 2000.

N.R. Madhava Menon (Ed.), The Legal Profession, 1984.

Nagel, Stuart S., The Legal Process from a Behavioural Perspective, 1969.

P.V. Kane, History of Dharamsastra, 1993 Reprint.

P.V. Young, Scientific Social Surveys and Research, 1977.

Palkhiwala, Nani A., We the Nation, 1994.

Palkhiwala, Nani A., We the People, 1997.

Rajiv Dhavan and Thomas Paul, Nehru and the Constitution, 1992.

Report of the National Commission to Review the Working of the Constitution, 2002.

Report: Cost of Litigation, 1988.

Report: Formation of an All India Judicial Service, 1986.

Report: Gram Nayalaya, 1986.

Report: Manpower Planning in Judiciary: A Blue Print, 1987.

Report: Method of Appointments to Subordinate Courts/ Subordinate Judiciary, 1986.

Report: Resource Allocation for Infrastructural Services in Judicial Administration..., 1988.

Report: The High Court Arrears—A Fresh Look,1988

Report: The Judicial Officers' Protection Act, 1850 1984.

Report: Urban Litigation Mediation as Alternative to Adjudication, 1988.

Robert Bierstedt, The Social Order, 1970.

Rocher, Ludo, Vacaspati Mishra "Vyavaharac-Intamani", A Digest on Human Legal Procedure, 1956.

Role of the Legal Profession in Administration of Justice, 1988.

Roman Services *v.* Subhash Kapoor, A.I.R. 2001 S.C. 207.

Ronald Irving, The Law is a Ass, 2002.

S.P. Gupta *v.* Union of India, 1981 Supp. S.C.C. 87.

Seervai, H.M., The Seervai Legacy..., 2001.

Sen Gupta, Naresh Chandra, Evolution of Ancient Indian Law, 1950.

Setalvad, Motilal C., My Life: Law and other Things, 2003.

Simon James, *et.al.* (Ed.), A Dictionary of Legal Quotations, 1996.

Singh, Nagendra, Justice Concepts of Ancient Indian Polity.

Sorabjce, Soli J., Law and Justice: An Anthology, 2003.

Stychin, Carl F., *et. al.*, Legal Method: Text and Material, 2003.

Supreme Court Bar Association *v.* Union of India, A.I.R. 1998 S.C. 1895.

The Daily Excelsior, 17.6.2003.

The Hindu, 24.9.2203 and Sep. 2002.

The Hindustan Times, 24.9.2003.

Training of Judicial Officers, 1986.

Union of India *v.* Bonnerjea (1995) 6 SCC 765.

Upendra Baxi, The Crisis of the Indian Legal System, 1982.

Wallace Mendelson (Ed.), Supreme Court Statecraft,1987.

William Shakespeare, King Lear.

William Shakespeare, The Merchant of Venice.

Index